Pictograph to Alphabet—and Back

Reconstructing the Pictographic Origins
of the Xajil Chronicle

Pictograph to Alphabet— and Back

Reconstructing the Pictographic Origins of the Xajil Chronicle

Robert M. Hill II

American Philosophical Society
Philadelphia • 2012

Transactions of the
American Philosophical Society
Held at Philadelphia
For Promoting Useful Knowledge
Volume 102, Part 4

ISBN: 978-1-60618-024-2

US ISSN: 0065-9746

Library of Congress Cataloguing-in-Publication Data

Hill, Robert M., 1952-
    Pictograph to Alphabet- and Back : Reconstructing the Pictographic
Origins of the Xajil Chronicle/ Robert M. Hill II, American
Philosophical Society.
        pages cm. — (Transactions of the American Philosophical Society :
Held at Philadelphia for Promoting Useful Knowledge ; Volume 102,
Part 4)
    Includes bibliographical references and index.
    ISBN 978-1-60618-024-2
    1. Cakchikel language—Writing. 2. Picture-writing, Indian.
3. Cakchikel language—History. 4. Cakchikel Indians—Social conditions.
5. Symbolism in communication. I. Title.
    PM3576.Z77I155 2012
    497'.42211—dc23
                        2012041065

Contents

Preface

The roots of this study grew many years ago during my undergraduate years at the University of Pennsylvania. I was always puzzled by the sudden shift of format and content in the document known at the time as "The Annals of the Cakchiquels," and that I shall refer to here more precisely as the "Xajil Chronicle." The Chronicle presented a lengthy record of ancestral migration in a timeless context. This account was suddenly replaced by a precise, year-by-year description of important events in the history of the Kaqchikel polity, from the 1490s through the early seventeenth century. Many years and other projects passed until Judith Maxwell and I collaborated on a fresh translation of the Xajil Chronicle, eliminating many errors and much confusion that had resulted from previous translations.

In the interim, students of Mesoamerican pictographic writing had defined a number of formal genres of preconquest indigenous historical documents with wide geographical and chronological distribution. I was particularly fortunate to have Elizabeth Hill Boone as a colleague at Tulane. It is safe to say that many of my insights into the Xajil Chronicle were inspired by her work.

It gradually became clear to me that the content of the Xajil Chronicle must have come from two different genres of now-lost pictographic documents: a so-called pictographic history and a continuous-year annal. The change in format and content that had puzzled me so long ago could now be explained as a shift from one genre of pictographic history to another.

The question became: how to prove it? Fortunately, work with Maxwell on the fresh translation of the Xajil Chronicle forced me to examine in minute detail the structure of the original Kaqchikel text. As a result, I stumbled on a hitherto undetected system of elaborate subheadings that I argue reflects the formal verbal recitation of the ancient pictographic texts.

The argument, evidence, and implications of this discovery appear herein.

Acknowledgments

I am delighted to thank the many individuals who made this work possible. Elizabeth Boone and Judith Maxwell made many comments and suggestions to early, faltering drafts. Christine Hernández scanned and edited the illustrations under my direction. Jane Hickman of the University of Pennsylvania Museum, kindly provided me with the images from Iximche' that appear in Figure 1.1. Nancy M. Shawcross, Curator of Manuscripts, Rare Book & Manuscript Library of the University of Pennsylvania, generously supplied the image of the manuscript used on the cover and in Chapter 2. Pierina Piedrasanta of the Universidad Francisco Marroquín went to extraordinary lengths to provide me with images of the Lienzo Quauhquechollan, a detail of which appears as Figure 7.3. Pamela Lankas, editor at IGS, offered support through the editorial and production process. Finally, special thanks to Mary McDonald, Director of Publications for the American Philosophical Society, for shepherding this work through to completion.

1

Introduction

THIS VOLUME IS AN ATTEMPT TO "upstream" from the alphabetic text of the longest and topically most diverse of the colonial Kaqchikel–Maya histories, the Xajil Chronicle, to determine the range of pictographic documents from which it might have been redacted. Most scholarship has proceeded the other way, working from the pictographic documents, attempting to decipher what they recorded. I have previously made a case that a significant part of the alphabetic text had been redacted from pictographic documents with origins firmly in the late preconquest highland Mesoamerican tradition (Hill 2005; Maxwell and Hill 2006, 13–15). I have even been able to make a strong case for the existence of a cartographic history (see Chapter 6) belonging to the Xpantzay, which they continued to update into the 17th century (Maxwell and Hill 2006, 20–21). If successful, we may gain insight into the range of documents that would have constituted a preconquest polity's historical "archive" and their different applications. We may also begin to gauge the quantity of information the pictographic documents intrinsically contained versus the amount of information an indigenous historian would have been required to memorize in order to interpret or perform them for others.

The Xajil, the Iximche' Policy, and the Chronicle

Because this information has been presented in other contexts (most recently in Maxwell and Hill 2006), only a summary will be provided here. The polity centered on the site of Iximche' was formed ca. 1470 when three Kaqchikel-speaking groups (the Xajil, Sotz'il, and Tuquche') split off from the regionally dominant K'iche'-Maya. One of the three groups (the Tuquche') was subsequently expelled from Iximche' by the other two and that year (1493) became the base date for the subsequent history of the polity as recorded in the Xajil Chronicle. The Xajil family gave its name to the group forming a dominant faction of the polity and was a "royal" line from which one of the two co-rulers of the

Iximche' polity was chosen. After the conquest the Spanish intentionally dismembered the polity and distributed its members among several new settlements created under the *congregación* program. Most of the Xajil family seems to have been assigned to the town of Solola', overlooking Lake Atitlan. Members of this branch of the Xajil family preserved, created, and presumably redacted the portions of the Xajil Chronicle that have come down to us. The Chronicle contains three distinct types of information: (1) the account of a long migration through which the Xajil and their allies arrived in highland Guatemala, (2) the genealogy and the careers of prominent ancestors, and (3) a year-by year account of important events in the history of the Iximche' polity that continued down through the early 17th century. I shall argue that these distinct genres of historical information correspond with preconquest pictographic formats and that subheadings in the presentation of the alphabetic text indicate that it was redacted from a range of pictographic accounts.

The Pictographic Tradition Among the Highland Maya

The first piece of the argument hinges on demonstrating that the late preconquest Kaqchikel (and, by extension, other K'ichean peoples) did indeed practice pictographic writing. Pictographic documents are associated with central and southern Mexico for the obvious reason that all of the surviving examples can be demonstrated to pertain to those regions. However, there is abundant evidence that the highland Maya shared in this tradition, which, in at least one instance, endured into the 17th century.

The earliest European reference is from Alonso de Zorita, who as a royal judge of New Spain visited Guatemala on several occasions, the earliest being ca. 1555 (Keen 1971, 34). He described specifically his visit to the K'iche' capital, Utatlan (Q'umarkaaj), where, as part of his enquiry into the political organization and mode of succession in the polity, he wrote:

I learned by way of their paintings which they had of their history for more than eight hundred years and which were interpreted for me by very old Indians, that in their pagan days they had three lords. The principal lord [as depicted?] had three fine featherwork canopies or mantles over his seat, the second had two, and the third one.

... averigüé por las pinturas que tenían de sus antigüedades de más de de ochocientos años, y con viejos muy antiguos, que solía haber entre ellos en tiempo de su gentilidad tres Señores, y el principal tenía tres doseles ó mantas de pluma muy ricas en su asiento, y el segundo dos, y el tercero una ... (Zorita 1941, 204)

Unfortunately, he does not describe the documents beyond this.

At about the same time (1550) a land dispute had arisen between two factions of the former Chajoma' polity (to the east of Iximche'), which at the time of the conquest extended across the eastern half of the modern Department of Chimaltenango and the northern third of the Department of Guatemala (Hill 1996). The dispute arose as a result of the Spanish dismemberment of the polity, creating the new town of San Martín Jilotepéque west of the Pixcaya River, and the towns of San Juan and San Pedro Sacatepéquez on the east side. The Pixcaya River was ultimately agreed upon by all parties as the new boundary between San Martín and San Juan/San Pedro. The San Juan people created a map of their territory, evidently drawn for the purpose recording their newly defined boundaries, but did so within the preconquest cartographic tradition. The map was presented (and thus preserved) in early-eighteenth-century litigation. Significantly, neither the date, nor the authenticity of the map were ever challenged by the opposing party to the litigation. I have published the map elsewhere (ibid, 66). It is clearly a short-hand version of a cartographic document, presenting only boundary information in the form of a sequence of named places, written in Kaqchikel with Spanish characters, describing a circuit. Because many of these toponyms were the confluences of rivers, it was possible to identify many of them and thus delineate the territory defined by the map.

The next reference is slightly later, from 1563. At that time a dispute arose over succession to leadership between two factions of the Tz'utujil town of Santiago Atitlan, on the south shore of Lake Atitlan. As neutral parties, two Kaqchikel leaders of Tecpan Atitlan were consulted (Solola', on the north shore of the lake and the town where the Xajil Chronicle presumably was redacted and updated). One of these leaders was the Ajpop of the Xajil, Don Jorge (Kab'lajuj Tijax), who had held the office since his installation by conquistador Pedro de Alvarado in 1532. Don Jorge died two years after the dispute, in 1565. The other witness was identified as his brother, Don Pedro de Robles (who later served as an alcalde of Solola' in 1564 and 1567). The two men were asked to interpret:

> . . . two lienzos in which the natives of said town [of Santiago Atitlan] have painted their houses and antiquity of those who were caciques and principal men.

> . . . dos lienzos en que los naturales del dicho pueblo [de Santiago Atitlan] tienen pintados sus casas y antigüedad de los que eran caciques y principales. (quoted from Carrasco 1967, 320)

The lienzos reportedly contained the pictures of the supreme lord, the Aj[pop] Tz'ikinajay, together with another fifteen lords subject to him (ibid, 320).

It is important to note that all of these references precede the maps made as parts of the Relaciones Geográficas in the late 1570s–80s. In other words, these pictographic documents represent the indigenous tradition, and were not Spanish-inspired creations like many of the surviving cartographic histories of central Mexico.

Writing in the late 17th century, Guatemalan criollo historian Fuentes y Guzmán mentions several pictographic documents available to him but subsequently lost. In describing an account of the K'iche' of the Quetzaltenango area at the time of the Spanish conquest, Fuentes mentions as one of his sources:

> . . . an old painting of antiquity which is in the possession of one of the principal Indians of Ixtahuacan _ which states and is understood by means

of figures, registering the title and rank of each Ahau, bearing the penmanship
of the first Indians to write [alphabetically].

> ... una añeja pintura de su antigualla que está en poder de los indios
> principales de Ystaguacan [sic] _ que se declara y entiende por figuras, tiene
> la letra de los primeros indios que escribieron, asentado el título y dignidad
> de cada Ahau. (Fuentes y Guzmán 1972, tomo III, 93)

Carmack estimates that this document was included with a redacted
alphabetic version composed in 1568 (Carmack 1973, 72).

I have presented Fuentes's description of another cartographic
document and I made the case that it was produced by the Xpantzay
family of the Iximche' polity (Maxwell and Hill 2006, 20–21). Unfortunately, Fuentes does not hazard a guess as to its antiquity at the time
he wrote about it from memory in 1686 and attribes it to the K'iche'
rather than the Xpantzay (probably due to the fact he examined it a
quarter-century earlier and was writing from memory). On the other
hand, this is the most detailed of any colonial-period description of a
pictographic document from the Guatemala highlands and thus deserves
quotation *in extenso*:

> There came into my hands a manta that was drawn on one side with ancient
> images, that was brought to this city of Guatemala, on account of a land
> litigation of the Indians of the Quiché [sic], and thusly its content showed
> a variety of mountains and valleys in their [the Indians'] style: there were
> three figures of Indians in different clothing and drawn with different hands
> spread out among those places as the lords and owners of them; and their
> clothing and devices of their finery indicated their [lordly] descent; but in
> the center or middle of the manta, that would be about a vara and a third
> square, a meeting circle of all those personages represented in those sites;
> which meant to indicate an agreement and pact they made among them,
> concerning the division of that territory.
>
> But in one part that, by its style was very close to ours, bearing towards
> the south, there was contained a round valley, [and] seated in a chair, a
> figure like a royal personage, since it was covered with a kind of gold-colored
> garland, with some little points above the upper part of the band: and it
> was [drawn] thus because it [the round valley] was the territory pertaining
> to a great cacique; and it is noteworthy that, after the Spaniards' arrival,
> they [the Indians] added to and augmented this map with some things by
> those who first knew to understand and write our letters: and especially in

that which is shown there; this valley that don Pedro de Alvarado marked out for pasturing the horses of the army has a horse painted, with a tiny scrap of paper superposed, and written on it *Alvarado*; and in the same place, more to the lower part of the valley, as though to indicate a later time, is painted a cow, and another little paper that says thusly *Argueta*. Because the latter passed to the possession of someone named Argueta. (Fuentes y Guzmán 1972, tomo II, 72. Translation by the author, based on Maxwell and Hill 2006)

The Kaqchikel and the Mixteca–Puebla Style

What might have been the style in which the "three figures of Indians with different hands spread out" and "with their clothing and devices of their finery" were depicted? Archaeological evidence indicates that these depictions would most likely have been in the "Mixteca–Puebla Style" of the late preconquest period. As a result of the destruction of Iximche' during the Spanish conquest and centuries of subsequent deterioration, very little evidence of the Kaqchikel's graphic style survives and all of it was found in one structure, identified by the site's excavator as Temple 2 (Nance, Whittington, and Borg 2003, 54). The remains consist of "traces of ten polychrome wall murals, all with human figures. Because the outlines had been incised into the base clay [of the temple walls], he was able to record several of these figures accurately, and he reproduced three of these as line drawings" (ibid, 56). The style of these figures is firmly within the widespread late-preconquest style referred to as "Mixteca-Puebla" or the "International Style" (Guillemin and Anders 1965; Carmack 1979; Boone and Smith 2003; see Figure 1.1). Significantly, these remains pertain to the temple's penultimate construction phase, thereby significantly predating the arrival of the Spanish and their central Mexican allies in 1524 (Nance, Whittington, and Borg, 2003, 56). There is also clear evidence of the use of the same style by the K'iche' from their capital, Q'umarkaaj/ Utatlan, indicating that its use was not limited to the Kaqchikel among the highland Maya in late preconquest times (Carmack 1981, 297; see Figure 1.2).

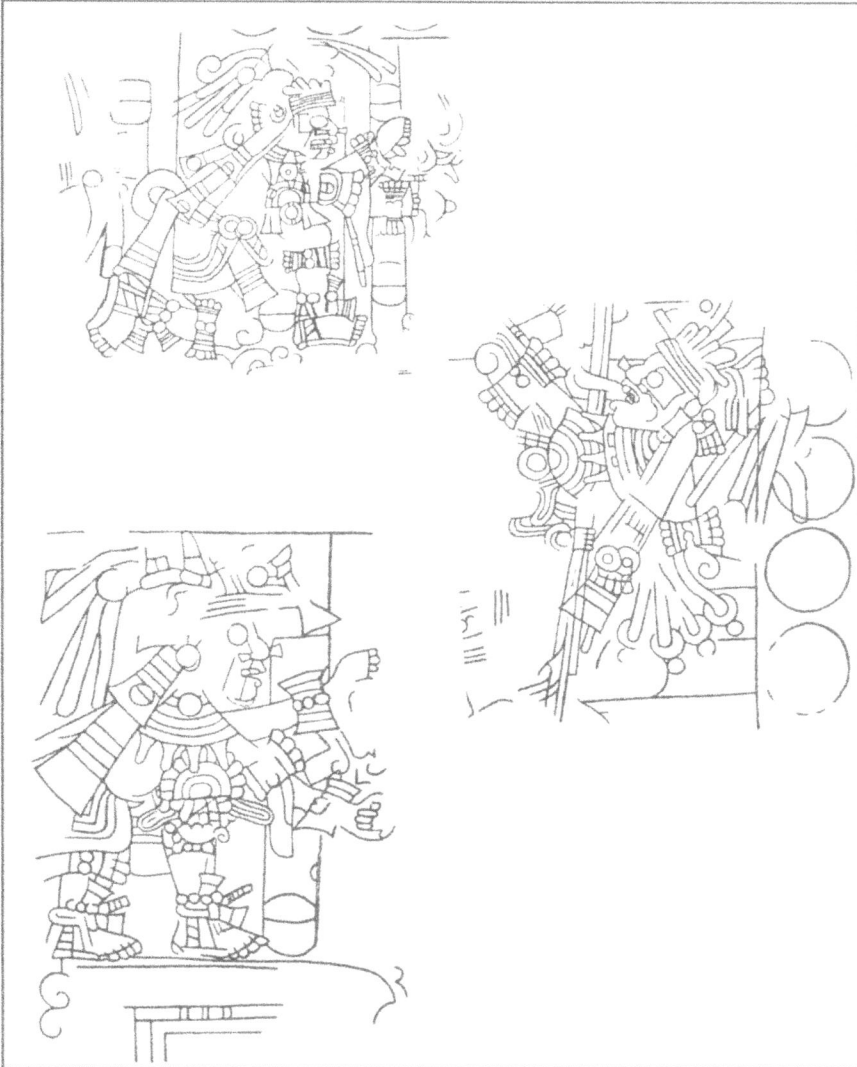

Figure 1.1 Images fron Iximche'.

Reproduced courtesy of the University of Pennsylvania Museum.

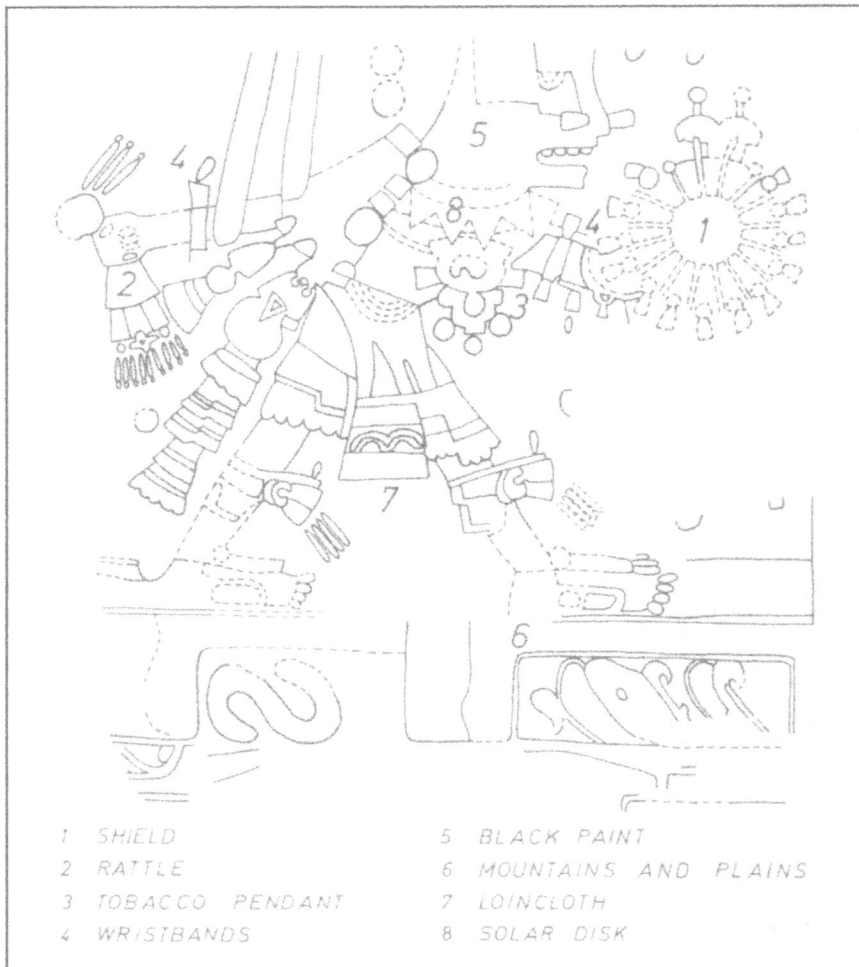

1 SHIELD   5 BLACK PAINT
2 RATTLE   6 MOUNTAINS AND PLAINS
3 TOBACCO PENDANT   7 LOINCLOTH
4 WRISTBANDS   8 SOLAR DISK

Figure 1.2   Image from Q'umarkaaj/Utatlan.

Reproduced from Carmack 1981, courtesy of the University of Oklahoma Press.

Pictographic Genres, Formats, and Implications

Boone has defined three main pictographic formats for the presentation of historical information in late-preconquest highland Mesoamerica:

(1) cartographic histories, (2) res gestae histories, and (3) continuous year-count annals (Boone 2000).

Cartographic histories employ a map format and stress the movement of people(s) through named locations. As a genre, the basic mode of presentation involves movement from one location to another, action at that location, and then movement to the next location as part of a long, elaborate series. The surviving cartographic histories are all of colonial manufacture and typically record a long period (though much of it indeterminable in purely chronological terms) from a group's origin, through its migrations, and down to its final establishment in its territory. However, there is no inherent reason why a cartographic format could not be used to record much shorter time periods. An important example here is the Lienzo of Quauhquechollan (Asselbergs 2004). In this case, an indigenous central-Mexican group of Spanish allies commissioned a large (3.25 x 2.45 m.) and pictographically dense cartographic history to record their participation in the conquest of Guatemala. Although it clearly records many places and events in that campaign, chronologically it covers a maximum span of only 10 years, from 1520 to 1529, though the focus by far is on just the two-year period of 1527–1529. The significance here is that there was no fixed time span to which a cartographic format was limited. Instead, its content could be dictated by the duration and density of the event(s) that its makers desired to record. I shall return to this implication when discussing the treatment of the Spanish conquest in the Xajil Chronicle (see Chapter 7). **The implication is that an elaborate movement–action–movement alphabetic text would likely have been redacted from a cartographic format.**

Res gestae or "accounts of deeds" is the only format for which we have examples of preconquest manufacture and all of these are associated with the Mixtecs. This does not imply, however, that the format was limited to those people. As a genre, res gestae stresses the careers of important individuals, their conquests, their marriages, and the genealogies of their descendants as a qualification for rulership. An important example for the present discussion is the Codex Bodley (see Boone 2000 for a useful summary). Apart from its specific content, one striking formal feature of the Bodley and others of this format is the emphasis on an individual character(s). Movement is decidedly secondary to both place and actor(s).

In this character-oriented context, we might logically expect that dialog (depicted by speech-scrolls coming from characters' mouths) would have been a prominent component of the history. We might further expect that much of the dialog, by necessity, would have been memorized by the indigenous historian and recited/performed before an audience, and there may have been subtle cues to content in the scenes themselves (Monaghan 1990, 1994; Troike 1982). However, direct quotation of speech acts is both sparse and terse in the res gestae sections of the Xajil Chronicle (these have been italicized in the text selections presented that follow for easier identification). In all of the accounts, speech is almost insignificant compared to place, action, and actor. Even a character's emotional state is described rather than revealed by his words. Indeed, the description of the emotional state provides the clue as to how the words are to be understood. **The implication here is that a character-oriented alphabetic text without the elaborate movement–action–movement format would likely have been redacted from a res gestae format.**

Continuous year-count annals (hereafter referred to as "annals") record important yearly events in the history of a polity, with its founding or some other political event as its starting point. The emphasis in this genre is on events in a specific year (though months might also be specified, see Chapter 6). The Codex Mexicanus and the Tira de Tepechpan are well-known examples of such annals. Years are typically identified by their name in the 52-year cycle, framed with a box or some other kind of visual division. A small pictograph denoting an important event is connected to the box by a line. For years with multiple events and/or a series of momentus years, multiple lines and pictographs result in a crowded, awkward presentation. Thus, a major limitation of this format is its inability to convey much detail about the events it records. **In any case, the implication here is that brief accounts of major events year by year in an alphabetic text would likely have been redacted from an annals format.** And indeed, we have examples of transitions between pictographic and alphabetic presentations in the annals format such as the Codex Aubin (see Chapter 8).

Because of the scarcity of examples of each format, some students of these annals seem to have interpreted them as stand-alone documents, with each individual document containing all of a particular polity's history. However, there is no inherent reason why any one of them could not have been supplemented by any of the other formats, which could provide much more detail about the events that another format could only hint at. To oversimplify using examples from our own historical genres, an annals format is analogous to a time-line presentation of the Napoleonic Wars. A cartographic history can be analogous to a treatment of a specific campaign or battle. A res gestae format is analogous to a biography of one of the important personages of the period. Boone has commented on the inherent strengths and limitations of the formats:

Each of these narrative forms . . . has different narrative strengths with concomitant weaknesses. The *res gestae* screenfold presents the personal details of dynastic history very efficiently as episodes in a series of episodes, but it does this at the expense of spatial relationships, notions of duration and continuity, and of presentational unity. The cartographic history gives simultaneity, spatial movement, and spatial relation at the expense of time. And the annals gives [*sic*] time above all, with its inherent qualities of continuity and duration, but cannot accommodate well the full details of person, place and event. (Boone 1994, 68)

I shall argue below that the Xajil Chronicle was derived from pictographic documents in all three formats. One of these was cartographic history that relates the travels of the Kaqchikel ancestors down to their arrival in Guatemala. Another document was a res gestae account that begins with the Twins' story and continues down to the Tuquche' revolt. The third was the annals section, which began as a traditional pictographic account and was supplemented by cartographic documents to record two preconquest battles and the unprecedented events of the Spanish conquest. Pictography in the annals was gradually supplemented and eventually supplanted entirely by alphabetic writing. The Xajil Chronicle conveys a vast and topically diverse range of historical information. In terms of the concerns of highland Mesoamerican history generally, it provides information on group origins and migrations, the careers of prominent individuals, their descendants, lines of rulership, and the chronology of important events in the history of an established polity. Indeed, the only topic not discussed in the Xajil Chronicle is territorial boundaries. Land and boundary information were of concern in other Kaqchikel documents (such as the 1555 Chajoma' map [p. 7] and the Xpantzay Cartulary), however. Accordingly, another assumption of the present exercise is that not one of these pictographic formats could conveniently convey enough of the relevant kinds of historical information contained in the Xajil Chronicle. Put another way, multiple formats and documents *must* have been employed to provide the range and quantity of information the Chronicle contains.

How did the pictographic documents of the Xajil Chronicle come to be redacted alphabetically? Available evidence points to the influence of 16-century Franciscan friars, Gonzalo Méndez in particular. In his massive *Crónica de la Provincia del Santísimo Nombre de Jusús de Guatemala* (an early-18th-century history of the Franciscan Order in Guatemala), Francisco Vázquez specifically credits Méndez as the force behind the creation of the Order's large collection of Kaqchikel-language documents, encouraging the literate Indians to write their traditional histories alphabetically:

> Already informed of many things of their paganism, and that a few knew how to write, he [friar Gonzalo] had them write their histories and titles, in their mode, in order that the world should know that they were rational [people], and to contradict the false opinion of some bigots, and in order that it be known that they were noble and brothers of the Spanish, all of them descendants of Adam and Eve.

> Ya enterado en muchas cosas de su paganismo, y que algunos sabían escribir, [fray Gonzalo] les hacía que escribiesen sus historias y títulos, a su

modo, para que supiera el mundo, que eran racionales, y deslumbrar la
impostura de algunos zoilos, y para que se conoce que eran nobles y hermanos
de los españoles, descendientes todos de Adán y Eva. (Vázquez 1938, 27)

Later in his history, Vázquez made it clear that he used a substantial
number of other Kaqchikel–Maya documents from the Order's archive:

. . . and it is recorded in the ancient papers of the Indians of said town
[Tecpan Guatemala], accounts like testaments (which, in their own language,
and translated, and explicated, I have and are kept with others in the archive
of this [Franciscan] Province) . . .

. . . consta de los papeles antiguos de dicho pueblo, así relaciones como
testamentos (que en su propio idoma, y traducidos, y explicados, tengo
presente y se guardan con los otros en el archivo de esta Provincia) . . . (Vázquez 1937, 21–22)

The impeccable penmanship in a single hand of the text of the
Xajil Chronicle that has come down to us is consistent with an unknown
friar having transcribed the collection of documents, probably in the
17th century.

2

Methods

I ARGUE HERE THAT EVIDENCE AS to the formats of the original pictographic documents and specific loci within them is contained both
in their topical content and in divisions of the text set off by an
elaborate scheme of **systematically employed** subheadings. Thus, a
further assumption is that these **subheadings are relics of the original
pictographic texts' first redaction** through verbal performance into
alphabetic form in the 16th century (the original text[s] of which have
not survived) and that the subheadings were not created/imposed by
the later, 17th-century transcriber of the alphabetic text that has come
down to us.

It might be countered that the elaborate subheading scheme simply
reflects the formal narrative style used in the performance of a **purely
oral** tradition rather than subdivisions of a pictographic text. Such an
argument is refuted by the following facts:

1. Evidence has already been presented in Chapter 1 to demonstrate
that the late preconquest K'ichean peoples of highland Guatemala partic-
ipated in the pictographic tradition.

2. We have evidence for the rendering of pictographic documents
in alphabetic form in some of the redactions themselves. As León-
Portilla notes in his analysis of the alphabetic Codex Chimalpopoca:

> In addition—and this is particularly important—the analysis permits us also
> to identify a good number of referential statements such as in *nican ca*, "here
> is"; *inin* . . . "this"; *iniqueh in*, "these . . . "; *inezca in nican an*, "of this, his
> appearance is here"; *izcatqui*, "here is . . . " such referential statements, accompa-
> nied by the frequent use of the adverbial phrases *niman ic, niman ye, niman ye
> ic*, menaning "then, next, following on," reveal that the text is being "read,"
> recited and committed to linear alphabetic writing, following the pictoglyphic
> [sic] sequences of an indigenous book. (Léon-Portilla 1992, 328)

Boone agrees for highland Mexico generally:

> Throughout the early alphabetic annals and histories there are references to
> older pictographic manuscripts from which the alphabetic texts were derived.
> The translators note that 'here is painted,' 'here it is noted,' 'as is shown in . . . '
> The textual histories are oral explanations of the paintings, transcribed alphabet-
> ically, but the chroniclers know that they are merely copying and filling in.
> (Boone 1998, 193)

There is an explicit statement to that effect in the Xpantzay Genealogy of Alonso Pérez in which he wrote: "As I am seeing it, thus I will write it down" (Maxwell and Hill 2006, 18). In Kaqchikel the verb "to see" //-tz'ët// is distinct from the verb "to read" //-sik'ij/. This lexical distinction strongly suggests that Don Alonso was looking at some kind of pictographic document, rather than referring to an alphabetic text, as he composed the genealogy (ibid, 18). Beyond this, the root for "read" also means "to call out or shout out to someone" (Maxwell, personal communication; Brown 1991). Thomás Coto, a 17th-century friar-linguist, noted this latter meaning; he glossed "llamar a voces" (shout out) as "çiqih" (Coto 1983, 32). These related meanings reinforce the performative aspect of reading, paralleling central Mexican practice.

3. It was precisely the oral performance that was being written down. We know from central- Mexican practice that such pictographic documents were "performed" as part of the education of young elites and perhaps as more public presentations as well. Indeed, the function of the pictographic documents was primarily as memory aides, thus requiring some form of verbal recitation to convey the more detailed accounts. In this context it would be counterintuitive to expect a divergence between oral performance and the alphabetic redactions. As Lockhart notes for the Nahua of central Mexico:

> Paradoxical as it may seem, the primary original purpose of alphabetic writing in the Nahua system of communication was to reproduce the oral component, and though things would change with time, this orality would always adhere to Nahua alphabetic documents more than to most comparable European texts. (Lockhart 1992, 335)

Four kinds of subheadings are present in the text and are illustrated from the first page of the Twins' Story (see Figure 2.1):

1. *Large subheadings*: These appear in bold, thick letters with capitals about 1.5 cm. tall. All save one begin with or contain the word "*Wa'e*" (or, in the other case, "*Wa*," which conveys the same meaning), indicating "Here." Our standard translation of these large

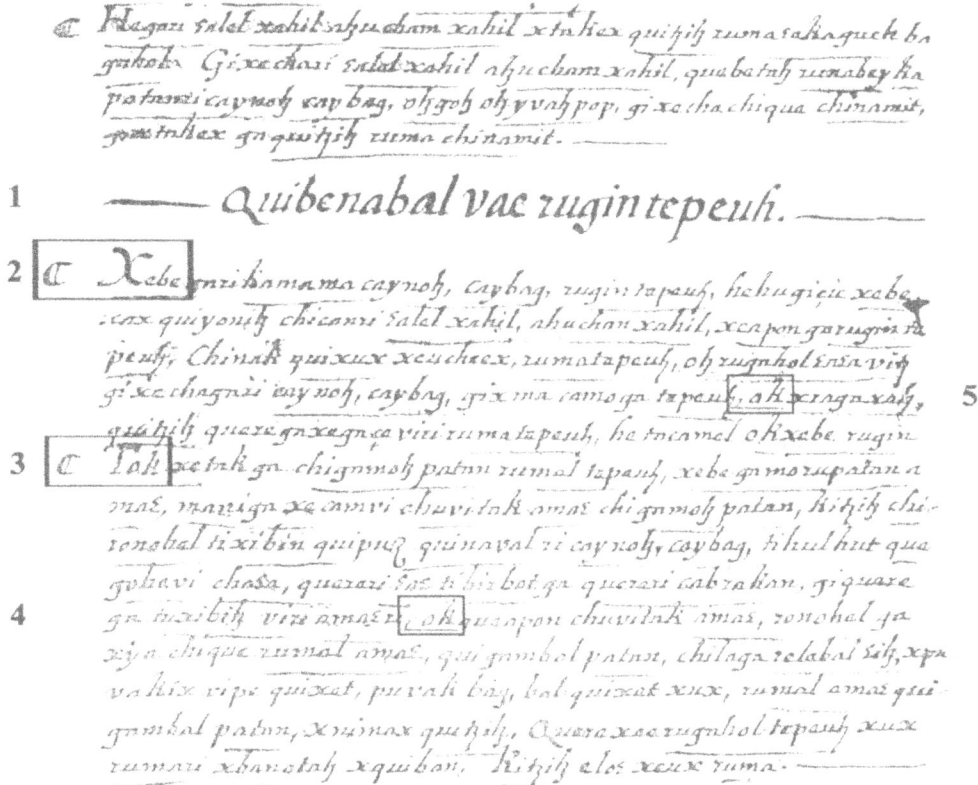

Figure 2.1   Types of subheadings from the beginning of the Twins' Story.
Reproduced courtesy of the Universiy of Pennsylvania Museum.

subheadings is "Presented Here," followed by the topic of the information or episode that follows.

2. *Small subheadings with serifs*: These consist of a paragraph
serif and a capital letter at the beginning of the first word. Because
capital letters are otherwise extremely rare in the text, their combination with the serif subheadings must indicate additional, significant
divisions of the textual material.

3. *Uppercase Töq/Öq subheadings*: These two words translate as
"then" or "when." They often appear with the serif, making them a

subset of *Small subheading*. They may occur within the text of a Small subheading. They are distinguished by the use of an upper case "T" or "Ö."

4. *Lowercase töq/ök preceeded by punctuation subheadings*: These also carry the meaning of "then." Though these are least prominent visually in the text, they appear systematically and logically at the beginning of even smaller episodes. Commas predominate overwhelmingly and periods very rarely occur. Technically, the commas and periods indicate the end of the previous phrase. A significant number of examples exist of *töq/öq without* the preceding comma. In these contexts their meaning is more properly "when," rather than "then." This difference in contextual usage demonstrates that the comma followed by *töq/öq* together has structural significance.

5. A complicating variant inovlves personal names that typically are followed by commas, which do not function as periods. A *töq/öq* following such a comma is more properly rendered as "when." A further complication is that punctuation, including commas, almost never occurs at the ends of sentences, again except after personal names. Thus, rarely, an *öq* may appear at the beginning of a sentence with a preceding comma if the previous sentence ended with a personal name. However, normally *öq* appears at the beginning of a sentence without a comma, thus making its function as a subheading ambiguous.

Two main lines of evidence point to the structural significance of all the *Töq/Öq* and *,töq/,öq* subheadings. First is their sheer frequency in the texts. Second, they function logically and systematically as lead-ins or transitions from one event/scene to another in a longer account. Both of these aspects are clearly seen when we use these subheadings as the basis for structuring the translation, as in the excerpt presented below.

In our translation, Maxwell and I asserted that the *Large subheadings with "Wa'e"* were performative deictics pertaining to discrete loci of a larger pictographic document, most likely a cartographic history (Maxwell and Hill 2006, 14). However, closer analysis of the organization and content of these passages suggests that the *Large subheadings with "Wa'e'* primarily indicate shifts from one large section of a pictographic document to another, such as the major sections of a map or a shift from one document format to another.

Our translation of the Chronicle employed a highly technical and complex interlinear format, for maximum transparency as to how we interpreted words and sentences. The details need not detain us here. An example of the format drawn from the beginning of the Twins' Story follows. When compared to the presentation organized by subheadings on pages 67–69, the difference is striking.

Kib'enab'al Wae' ruk'in Tepew

Ki-be-n-a-b'äl wa'-e' r-uk'in Tepew.
3Ep-go-sf-l-I-N Pd-D 3E-with Tepew
Here their journey to Tepew. [Note the use of the *Large subheading with Wa'e'* to indicate a new document or major shift in a longer document.]

¶ Xeb'e K'a ri' qamama Ka'i' Noj, Ka'i' B'atz' ruk'in Tepew.
Xb'e ka' ri' qa-mamá Ka'i' Noj Ka'i' B'atz' r-uk'in Tepew PS-3Ap-go
D D 1Ep-grandfather 2-CN No'j two CN B'atz' 3E- with Tepew
Our grandfathers Ka'i' Noj [and] Ka'i' B'atz' went to Tepew's.

Je' Juk'isïk xebe'; xa xkiyonij chi kan ri Q'alel Xajil, Ajuchan Xajil.
Je' ju-k'ïs-ïk x-0-b'e xa x-0-ki-yon-ij chi[k] kan ri Q'alel Xajil Ajuchan Xajil
D one-end-N PS-3Ap-go just PS-3A-3EP-alone-TR r remain D Q'alel Xajil Ajuchan Xajil
They went alone; they just remained alone, the Q'alel Xajil [and] the Ajuchan Xajil.

Xe'apon k'a ruk'in Tepew.

x-e'-apon k'a r-uk'in Tepew
PS-3Ap-arrive D 3E-with Tepew
They arrived before Tepew.

"Chi naq kixüx?," xe'uche'ëx ruma Tepew.
Chi naq K-ix-üx x-e'-uche'-ëx r-uma Tepew
PR D PRS-2Ap-be PS-3Ap-say-PV 3E-cause Tepew
"Who are you?" they were asked by Tepew.

"Öj ruk'ajol Q'aq'awitz," k'i xecha k'a ri' Ka'i' Noj Ka'i' B'atz'
Öj ru-k'-ajol Q'aq'awitz k'i x-e-cha k'a ri' Ka'-i' No'j Ka'I' B'atz'
1Ap 3E-son Q'aq'awitz D PS-3Ap-say D D two-CN No'j two-CN B'atz'
"We are the sons of Q'aq'awitz," this they said, then, Ka'i' Noj
[and] Ka'i' B'atz'.

K'i xmakamo k'a Tepew, öq xrak'axaj kitzij.
K'i x-0-makamo k'a Tepew öq x-0-r-ak'ax-aj ki tzij
D PS-3A-astound D Tepew when PS-3A-3E-hear-VT 3Ep-word
Then Tepew was astonished when he heard their words.
[Note the personal name followed by ,*ök*.]

Ke re' k'a xek'ase' wi ri' ruma Tepew.
Ke re' k'a x-0-k'as-e' wi ri' r-uma Tepew
D D D PS-3Ap-alive-IP TC D 3E-cause Tepew
Thus they were elevated by Tepew.

Je' ta kamel öq xeb'e ruk'in.
Je' ta kämel öq x-e-b'e r-uk'in
D neg die-AG when PS-3Ap-go 3E-with
They has been humble when they went to him.
[Note the *öq* without preceding punctuation.]

¶ Töq xetaq k'a chi k'amoj patan rumal Tepew.
töq x-e-täq k'a chi k'äm-oj patan r-umal Tepew
then PS3Ap-send D PR bring-N tribute 3E-cause Tepew
Then they were sent by Tepew to bring tribute.

[Note the serif followed by *Töq*. This indicates a new image or frame in the pictographic account.]

Although we reproduced faithfully the *Small subheadings with serifs* and the *Töq/Öq subheadings* throughout our interlinear-format translation, I admittedly paid less attention than I might have to their possible significance. With our emphasis on producing a translation that also captured the poetic quality of some parallelistic couplets, we were unsystematic in our interpretation of the *,töq/,öq subheadings* (though this does not affect the integrity of the translation as such). However, all of these smaller subheadings seem to have the deictic function that we originally attributed to the *Large subheadings with "Wa'e'."* In other words, it is the various Small subheadings that reflect discrete loci in larger documents to which the performer would point or refer while reciting the memorized content of the event. Such loci might be individual frames or sections in a res gestae account or a stopping point in a cartographic account where some significant action occurred. The *Small subheadings with serifs* undeniably reflect discrete loci in the annals format, in which they distinguish the different events that occurred in a given year (see Chapter 6).

The *Small subheadings with serifs* and *Töq/Öq subheadings* both would seem to work well in setting off pictographic loci in the context of the recitation of a lengthy cartographic history with its inherent succession of movement–event–movement. The *Töq/Öq* and *,töq/,öq* subheadings seem well suited to the sequential content of a frame or page in a biographical/genealogical res gestae format.

The placement of these different subheadings is not random, indicating that their use was not arbitrary on the part of the redactor but integral to the performance of the original pictographic texts. For example, *,töq/,öq* are rare in the annals format. Similarly, *Töq/Öq* subheadings are rare in the annals section, presumably because the events recorded in a given year are not causally related. Given these differential distributions of subheadings, it is possible to combine genre/content and subheading type/distribution to systematically differentiate the sub-divisions of the text and to suggest the type of pictographic document format(s) from which they were redacted:

Cartographic

Presentation: elaborate movement–action–movement sequence through space and time

Genre/Content: origin/migration-history of group

Subheadings: *Small subheadings*, including *Töq/Öq* with serifs

Res Gestae

Presentation: sequence of scenes stressing interaction among a small number of actors

Genre/Content: focus on individuals' political/military careers, marriages, and offspring

Subheadings: high frequency of *,töq/,öq subheadings* that open small episodes

Annals

Presentation: year-by-year, month-by-month list of events

Genre/Content: important events that occurred in a given year

Subheadings: *Large subheadings* for each year and *Small subheadings with serifs*, rarely including *Töq/Öq* with serifs for different events in a given year

Can these subheadings be correlated with scenes/episodes in surviving pictographic documents from other parts of highland Mesoamerica? I will argue that to some degree they can, though there are several important caveats to consider.

First, many of the surviving Mixtec screenfolds and central Mexican cartographic histories exhibit a concern with calendrical dates and absolute time. Although it may seem a strange thing to say about any Maya people, such a concern with dates is conspicuously absent from much of the Xajil Chronicle. The date of departure from Tulan is not given. None of the events in the migration led by Q'aq'awitz are dated, nor is the Twins' story. Indeed, prior to the Tuquche' revolt the only calendrical dates are: (1) the abandonment of Chi Awär, (2) the arrival at the resting place at Xe K'at B'a Yaki, and (3) the arrival at Ratz'amüt (where Iximche' was then founded). The immediately preceding episodes (the revolt against K'iqab') are not dated, nor are the deaths of any of the prior Kaqchikel rulers or the installation of their successors. After the Tuquche' revolt the annals section begins. Only at this point does time become the structure on which the reportage is presented.

Second, the Xajil make no claim to "Chichimec" origins as was normal for Nahua-speakers from central Mexico. In the case of the latter, much of their early history is conveyed in cartographic format, with the people depicted in clothing of shaggy skins, as befits their original "un-civilized" status. Only later, as they become civilized through contact with settled, urban descendants of the Toltecs, do they appear in the cotton clothing of "civilized" peoples. In contrast, the Xajil story begins with the departure of the highland Maya peoples from Tulan. They are not uncivilized, and upon their departure they are invested with the accouterments of Mesoamerican "high" civilization and receive the injunction to set off to find (and conquer) their ultimate homes. Their journey consists primarily of overcoming topographic and military challenges, rather than passing out of "barbarism." Accordingly, we would expect the figures in a cartographic account drawn by the Kaqchikel to be uniformly in Mesoamerican costume and rendered in the Mixteca–Puebla style (as suggested previously). Although there are no surviving preconquest examples of a migration account in the Mixteca–Puebla style, we have several postconquest lienzos in cartographic format in that style in which we can see the same movement–action–movement presentation of the Nahua accounts.

Third, all of the surviving pictographic accounts from the Valley of Mexico were produced after the Spanish conquest. Although we assume that these documents reflect preconquest formats and genres, many exhibit combinations of these that suggest a degree of blending of several different genres of indigenous documents into single, synthetic accounts. One motivation for this could have been the Spanish destruction of the indigenous originals and the desire on the Nahuas' part to salvage as much information as possible as quickly as possible, before memory of their contents faded. Some of these may have been produced at least partly for more prosaic purposes, such as evidence for litigation in Spanish courts (Leibsohn 2009). By the 1570s the Spanish program of Relaciones Geográficas probably also resulted in combined formats and genres as means for the indigenous groups to supply the required information in an economical format (Robertson 1972).

The final caveat concerns the completeness of the redactions in the Xajil Chronicle. Even if all of the assumptions presented here are correct, we cannot determine whether the complete contents of all the pictographic accounts were redacted, or if instead they were recounted selectively according to unknown criteria at the time. There are two pieces of evidence to suggest that some accounts may have been edited. The weaker of these is the brevity of some accounts under the *Large subheadings with Wa'e'*. As already noted, these subheadings are assumed to represent either an entire document or large sections of one. A brief account under one of these subheadings inherently suggests some suppression of detail. A stronger piece of evidence comes from the Xajil Chronicle itself. Near the end of the account of Q'a'qawitz's sister (see p. 63) we find the statement: "There is more [of this story] that we will not enter." The implication is that the original redactor decided not to include additional information (and conceivably quite a lot of it) in order to proceed to the next major document, which I believe to have been a res gestae account.

With all these caveats in mind, the criteria outlined earlier can be used to differentiate sections of the Xajil Chronicle. Illustrative excerpts of the Xajil Chronicle appear below. The major divisions of the entire Chronicle and their presumed formats are listed here:

Ms. pages	18–27	Primary cartographic account of migration from Tulan.
Ms. pages	27–33	Episodic cartographic accounts of Q'aq'awitz in the volcano, the sacrifice of Tolk'om, and Q'aq'awitz's sister.
Ms. pages	34–45	Res gestae accounts, including genealogical passages.
Ms. pages	45–46	Cartographic account of battle against the K'iche.'
Ms. pages	46–47	Res gestae accounts of deaths of Ich'al and K'awoq.
Ms. pages	48–49	Cartographic account of the Tuquche' revolt.
Ms. pages	50–56	Beginning of annals format.
Ms. pages	56–59	Cartographic account of Spanish conquest.
Ms. pages	59–92	Return to annals format.

A Note on Excerpts and Images

I will present excerpts of varying length from the text of the Chronicle to achieve several ends. Foremost, the excerpts will provide readers unfamiliar with the Chronicle with specific examples of the different genres and a subjective "feel" for their varying content. Even readers familiar with the Maxwell and Hill translation will be able to see the narrative structure of the passages more clearly. Second, extended excerpts also provide some insight into the performative aspect of the texts. Many of these accounts were not brief and the recitation of them undoubtedly would have been a lengthy affair. Third, based on the case I have made regarding the relationship between *Small subheadings* and discrete loci or images in a larger document, the extended excerpts also suggest how many pictographs might have been needed as prompts to convey the different kinds of information. Finally, the extended excerpts, when combined with the images gleaned from other pictographic texts, suggest the quantity of information that would have required memorization by an indigenous historian.

In a few instances, based on the action described in a section of the Xajil Chronicle, I have included images taken primarily from the Codex Zouche–Nuttall (henceforth, CZ–N) (Nuttall [1902]1975). My attempt here is **only** to suggest the potential of the Mixteca–Puebla Style of representation to have conveyed the information contained in the different genres, or at least prompting a narrator already well versed in their contents. The number of images used is necessarily limited to those that depict scenes in some way similar to a specific subsection of the Chronicle. However, I do not intend to suggest that the Zouche–Nuttall accounts are in any way parallel to any specific portion of the Xajil Chronicle. I have taken the liberty of editing out the names of the personnages from the images. They occupy a great deal of space in the scenes and might otherwise be a distraction for those not familiar with the conventions of the Mixteca–Puebla Style. Deleting names also decontextualizes the images from their conventional interpretations by scholars, thereby making the images more generic in nature.

I stress that these images are only examples to **suggest** how the prompt to the succeeding passage(s) **might** have looked. The total number of images undoubtedly would have been substantially greater. For example, the number of various kinds of Small subheadings in the relatively brief res gestae portion of account of the Twins, Ka'i' Noj and Ka'i' B'atz, suggests that as many as 13 images might have been employed. By the same criteria, the brief excerpt from the cartographic account that will be presented could have had 12 images. The long excerpt from the events during the leadership of Q'aq'awitz and Sak-tekaw could have involved 30 images. The actual number of images involved might have been somewhat fewer, depending on the number of figures grouped in a particular scene. Thus, in the cartographic account presented below, a scene with multiple characters (such as the one in Figure 3.1, p. 36, excerpted from the Codex Zouche–Nuttall) might have sufficed for several succeeding Small subheadings, as the reciter pointed to each individual figure in turn, identifying them for his audience.

I have also included a few edited scenes abstracted from the Historia Tolteca–Chichimeèa, Mapa Sigüenza, Lienzo de Quauhquechollan, and Codex Aubin to suggest how pictographic texts from different genres might have been used in different portions of the Xajil Chronicle.

3

Cartographic Migration Account

THIS SECTION OF THE XAJIL CHRONICLE begins with a *Large subheading with Wa'e'* on page 18 of the original manuscript and continues without any additional Large subheadings until the death of Saktekaw on manuscript page 27. This represents an enormous amount of textual space and information. The number of images and the physical size of the map that contained them both would have been massive. Some idea of the document's size is suggested by the Lienzo of Zacatepec (Smith 1973). Created by the Mixtecs of the town of Santa María Zacatepec in the mid-sixteenth century, this cartographic document was drawn on three strips of cotton cloth sewn together. The overall dimensions of the resulting lienzo were an impressive 3.25 by 2.25 meters (ibid, 88–93).

Q'aq'awitz and Saktekaw (until his death) are the focus of most of the action in the Xajil Chronicle. They represent (metaphorically and, most likely, graphically as well) an entire migrant people. They interact with other characters, many of whom, likewise, represent entire peoples. Q'aq'awitz ultimately founds a dynasty, that of his Kaqchikel descendants. The entire account is tied to the movement–action–movement presentation of a cartographic format. The account of the peoples' arrival at the seaside contains much dialog that probably could not have been conveyed pictographically, except for speech-scrolls to indicate that dialog was occurring. Accordingly, this passage is presented in extenso to give some indication of the kind and amount of information that a reciter would need to have memorized.

Excerpt from Maxwell and Hill (2006, 19–27).

¶ The Seven Amaq's first came here from Tulan, they say.
  We came last, we, the warriors.
  All the Seven Amaq's [and] the warriors were bringing their
    burdens when (töq) the entrance to Tulan was opened.
  It was the Tz'utujils who were the first of the Seven Amaq's,
    when (öq) they came from Tulan.

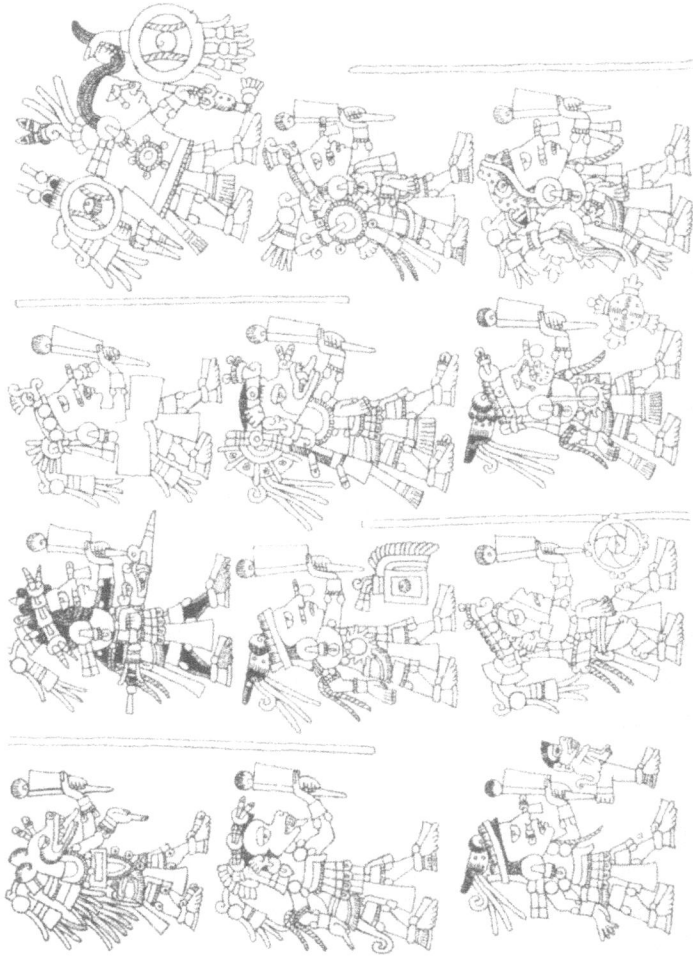

Figure 3.1 This image from the CZ-N (Nuttall [1902] 1975, page 76) actually represents a ritual procession. It is used here to suggest how a series of individuals, representing different peoples, might have been portrayed. Given the density of representation, this series of individuals might have been used to prompt this section of six *Small subheadings*.

Reproduced courtesy of Dover Publications, New York.

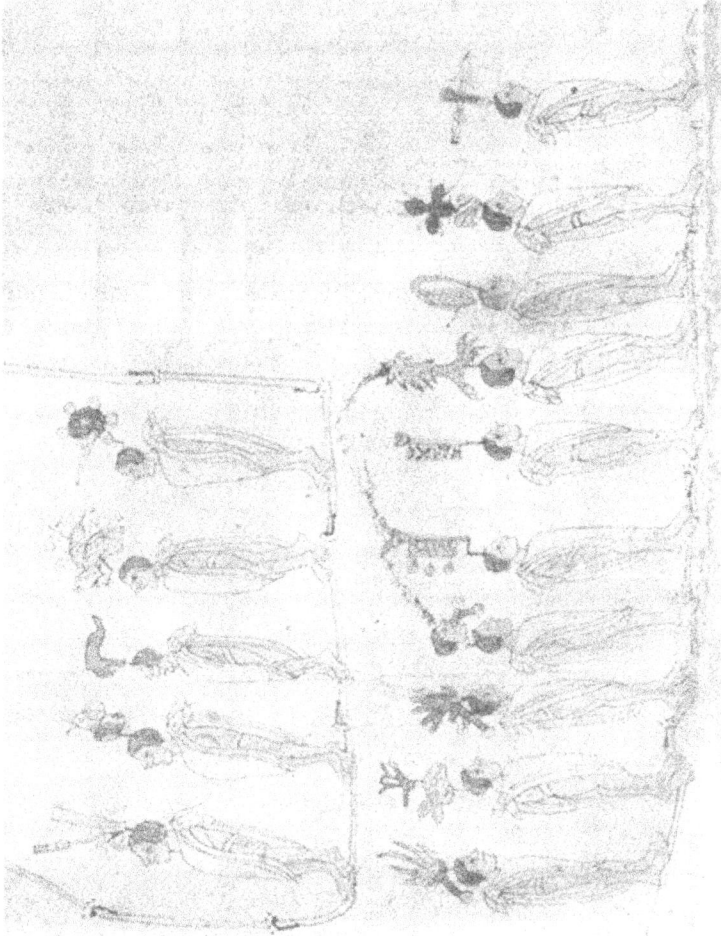

Figure 3.2 This edited detail from the Mapa Sigüenza (Casteñeda de la Paz 2006) is drawn in a postconquest, European-influenced style. It depicts the beginning of a migration account and, again, suggests how individual figures could have represented entire peoples.

Reproduced courtesy of the Instituto Nacional de Antropología e Historia.

37

Once the Seven Amaq's had finished coming, immediately there-
after we came, we, the warriors, they say.

Our mothers, our fathers spoke forth when (öq) we were counseled thus: *"Go forth, you, my daughters, you my sons!*

I will mete out your wealth, your lordship.

I will mete out your power, your majesty.

You the canopy, you the throne.

Therefore, you will bear these: rounded wood, straight cane;
        arrows, shields; bright feathers, white clay.

If you should carry jade, precious metal, quetzal [and] raxom
        feathers; and if you will carry writings [and] carvings; 260-day
        calendars, solar calendars; flutes [and] songs, let you not be disre-
        spected for that!

Rather, that which the Seven Amaq's bore will be yours.

May you carry it there! May you take possession of it! May you dis-
        play it!

I have not yet meted out their lordship.

Rather, you will bear it; truly great will be your destiny.

May you never be disrespected, but rather may you become great!

These rounded wood, straightened cane.

Do not sleep, do not be defeated there, you, my daughters, you, my sons!

I will mete your lordship, you, thirteen ajpops.

May you test your arrows, your shields, your lordship, your canopy,
        your throne!

Thus these are your elders," the K'iche' Winäq were told.

Then (,öq) the thirteen divisions of warriors came hither from Tulan.

So, first came the K'iche' Winäq.

The flaying [ritual] of Tlacaxipehualistli was the burden of the K'iche'
        Winäq when (öq) they came hither, accompanied by the various
        houses, chinamïts, limbs of the amaq', each division of warriors.

Then (,töq) they came hither from Tulan when (öq) they [the K'iche']
        all had finished coming forth:

¶ The Rabinals came, the Sotz'il people came, the Tuquche' came, the
  Tujalaljay, the Uchab'ajay, those of Ch'umilajay [came].
The Lamaq's [and] Kumätz came also.
The Aqajal people and those of Tukur came also.
All this coming forth ended.

Then (,Töq) the thirteen divisions of warriors also came: we, the B'akaj
  Poq; we the B'akaj Xajil.

One came first; the other, which belonged to us, came last.
The first B'akaj, the B'akaj Poq thus came first.
We came next, we, we, the B'akaj Xajil, said they, our grandfathers,
  you, our sons.
Earlier came the Seven Amaq's, earlier the warriors began to come.

Then (Töq) we came, we, the Kaqchikel people.
  "It is true that we came hither from Tulan last.
  There was no one left when we came," said Q'aq'awitz [and] Saktekaw.
  We were counseled: *"These are your chinamïts,"* the Q'eqak'üch, the
    B'ak'ajol, the Sib'aqijay were told.
  *"These are your two Ajpops: one [the] ajpop the other [the] ajpop
    k'amajay, for them,"* the Q'eqak'üch, B'ak'ajol, [and] Sib'aqijay
    were told.
  "May you receive your ajpops!" they were told.
  Thus, these are the mothers, these are the affines who were first.
  And so first came the Sib'aqijay, then came the B'ak'ajol, then came
    the Q'eqak'üch.
  First came these chinamïts.

Figure 3.3   This image from the CZ–N (Nuttall [1902] 1975, page 14) suggests how the account of the arrival at the seaside and subsequent action under the *.Öq subheading* below might have been prompted. Notice that the figures carry staves, perhaps analogous to the one used by the Kaqchikel to part the ocean.

Reproduced courtesy of Dover Publications, New York.

Excerpt from Maxwell and Hill (2006, 35–57).

Then (.Öq) we arrived at the seaside.
    They were already there; all the amaq's, all the warriors, were
        gathered by the seaside when (öq) we encountered them.
    Their hearts were finished [discouraged].
    *They have nothing with which to cross over; no manner of crossing
        has been told,"* said all the warriors [and] the Seven amaq's
        to us.

"Whom may we call? With what shall we cross?

You, our younger brothers, we were waiting just for you," they all said.

We said to them: *"Console yourselves, you, our elders!*

With what shall we cross now that we are all here?" we said.

Immediately all of them said: *"Take pity on us, you, our younger brothers!*

Just let us collapse here at the waterside, at the sea!

We have not yet found our hills, our plains!

Instead, soon we will sleep, soon we will be beaten!

We are two of the children; we are the top, we are the head; we are the first warriors, the Seven amaq's, you, my younger brother.

If we were to cross, we would soon see the face of our burden that was given to us by our mothers, our fathers, you, my younger brother," said to us those who sired the K'iche' people, said our grandfathers Q'aq'awitz [and] Saktekaw.

We said to them: *"Let us try, you our older brothers!*

Let us not stay here, let us not lie down here along the seashore!

It shall not be! We have not yet discovered our territory. It does exist.

It is said that you will see it, you warriors, you Seven amaq's!

Let us cross now!" we said.

Immediately, they all rejoiced.

"A red tree was our standard when (öq) we came; we brought it over from the entrance of Tulan.

Thus we are named the Kaqchikel People, you, my sons!" said Q'aq'awitz [and] Saktekaw.

Just the base of our standard was stabbed into the sand, in the sea.

Immediately, the sea was split by the sand.

Indeed, the red tree which we brought forth from the entrance of Tulan was necessary.

We crossed over on a path of sand when (öq) the bottom of the ocean almost became the surface of the sea.

Immediately, then (öq), everyone rejoiced when they saw the sand in the sea.

Immediately, they conferred: *"There let us await each other, atop the first hill; there let us gather together!"* they said.

Thus was our ordering when we came from Tulan.

They tumbled forth; they crossed over the sand.

And so it was that we came from the sea at last; we emerged from the water's edge.

But soon, all the Seven Amaq's became frightened; so said all the warriors when (öq) the Seven amaq's said: *"Only this, which you saw, is our burden.*

We have exalted it with you, you lords, you warriors!

But let us not go to the east with you!

Rather, we will look for our hills, our plains.

Only this is our burden which you saw: quetzal feathers, raxom feathers, trogon Feathers," said the Seven Amaq's.

They conferred: *"Very well,"* the Seven Amaq's were told.

Thus, their council ended.

Figure 3.4 This CZ–N image (Nuttall [1902] 1975, page 39) suggests how the passage over mountains in the following *,ōk Small subheading* portion of the excerpt might have been prompted. At least four additional images would have been needed to indicate all of the mountains named in the entire excerpt.

Reproduced courtesy of Dover Publications, New York.

Then (,ök) they came over the hill, Teosakwanku.

Later they came over another hill named Me'ajaw.

There atop it, they gathered themselves.

They left from there, from the summit of Me'ajaw.

They arrived at the summit of the hill named Walwal Xukxuk.

There, atop it, they rested.

They gathered themselves yet again; they left from there.

Next they arrived at the summit of the hill named Tapku Oloman.

They all gathered again there; we held council atop it there.

Said our fathers Q'aq'awitz [and] Saktekaw: *"Not until that place did we adorn ourselves; and there did we untie our burden."*

All the warriors said: *"What should we do?*

These are our identities here: we, those of obsidian, those of rope; we the displayers of our burden, you, our younger brother; you, our older brother," they said to us.

We told them: *"Our battle is now near. So, let us adorn ourselves, let us bedeck ourselves, let us don feathers, let us untie our burden!*

We have our burden, given to us by our mothers, our fathers.

Let us don feathers! I am the one that knows!" we said to them.

Then (,öq) all of us came, each division on its route.

These were their paths when (öq) they returned to the top of the hill, Walwal Xukxuk:

They passed over the hill named Meme' Juyu', Takna Juyu'.

They arrived at the summit of the hill named Saqitew, Saqik'uwa'.

They came forth over the summit of Me'ajaw, Kuta'm Chäj.

From there they returned hither over the hill named Saqijuyu'.

Tepakuman.

Then (töq) they passed over to see their mountains, their plains.

Then (,öq) they passed over the hill, Tojojil; the K'iche' people dawned there.

They passed Pantzik.

"At Pa Raxon we dawned, you, my sons." they said, they, our first
    fathers, our grandfathers, Q'aq'awitz [and] Saktekaw.
These are the hills, the plains which they crossed, they circled.
Lest our exaltation end, we proclaimed our territory.
Let us not forget that, truly, through many hills we passed," said
    our grandfathers long ago.

¶ These are the hills where they passed:
From above Popo' Ab'äj, they descended on Ch'opitzel, Pa Nima-
    k'oxom [and] Xe Nimachäj.
They descended there at Muqulïk Ya' [and] Molomïk Che'.

4

Res Gestae Account of Q'aq'awitz

ADDITIONAL *Large subheadings with Wa'e'* occur over another seven manuscript pages that refer to Q'aq'awitz's death on page 33 and the miraculous appearance of his twin sons on page 34. These subheadings probably represent shifts to another document, probably in res gestae format, as the episodes of Q'aq'awitz in the volcano, the sacrifice of Tolk'om, and Q'aq'awitz's sister are filled with detail and dialog that would heve been difficult to record in the context of the larger cartographic account found on manuscript pages 18–27. These episodes are presented below to suggest the length and complexity of the original pictographic document. As noted previously, on manuscript page 31, the episode of Q'aq'awitz's sister ends with the statement: "There is more here that we will not enter," which we have interpreted as an indication that there is more to the account/text but that it is not all being written down.

Excerpt from Maxwell and Hill (2006, 82–91).

Figure 4.1   This image from the CZ–N (Nuttall [1902] 1975, page 14) suggests how the ravine crossing episode in the next two *Small subheadings* (one with serif, the other, *,öq*) might have been depcited. Another image would have been needed for the subsequent *Small subheading with serif*.

Reproduced courtesy of Dover Publications, New York.

The Victory of our Grandfathers. Then (,öq) he Died

¶ They arrived at the Ch'opitzel Hill.

    Q'aq'awitz said to Saktekaw: *"Let us cross the ravine!"*

"*Very well,*" he [Saktekaw] said.
Q'aq'awitz crossed first.

Then (,öq) Saktekaw tried to cross.
He did not make it.
He fell into the ravine.
Thus one of our grandfathers died.
They were separated.
The other one engendered us, we the Xajils.

¶ They arrived again atop the hills Saqijuyu' and Teyokuman
      at twice their distance.
There they saw the fire of the mountain maned Q'aq'xanul.
The fire coming from inside the mountain was truly frightening.
For one year the mountain, Q'aq'xanul, had fire.
Never before had fire come out. All the warriors, The Seven
      Amaq's had arrived at the foot of the mountain.
They were saying nothing.
Truly their hearts were pained until the taking of the fire
      was discussed.
"*Let us just go, let us go with confidence,*" said our grandfa-
      ther Q'aq'awitz.
They arrived at the foot of the mountain.
All the warriors said: "*You, our younger brother have arrived;
      you whom we were waiting for.
Who will announce the bringing of our fire?
We have tried. Try your fortune, you, our younger brother,*" all
      of them said.
We said to them: "*Who wishes it? Let me stay and try it yet!
Whoever has a brave heart, let him not be frightened. I will lead
      the way!*" said Q'aq'awitz to them.
Nobody wanted [to go].
Soon they were frightened.
The fire of the mountain was in truth frightening.

Figure 4.2   In this image from the CZ–N (Nuttall [1902] 1975, page 66) the smaller figure on the right is actually part of the larger figure's personal name. It is used here to suggest how characters of unequal status might have been portrayed as a prompt for the next *,öq Small subheading*. Two additional images would have accompanied the two subsequent Small subheadings.

Reproduced courtesy of Dover Publications, New York.

Then (,öq) one whose name was Saqitz'unun wanted [to go].
"*Let me go with you,*" said Saqitz'unun to Q'aq'awitz.

Then (,töq) both of them adorned, bedecked, made themselves
beautiful, but not with arrows, with shields.
    They just stripped, and splinted [themselves with] reeds called
        green cane.
    It was with plants coming from the water that they
        adorned themselves.
    It covered their hair, it covered their necks, their elbows, their
        arms, their legs.
    "*It is a killer for fire,*" they said.
    Q'aq'awitz descended into the fire.
    Saqitz'unun remained watering the flames.
    Green corn was dissolved in water which was poured on
        the flames.
    In truth, it was frightening when he descended inside the
        mountain.

Then (,öq) the fire of the mountain was shattered.
    Its smoke spewed afar.
    Darkness, night entered.
    All who were at the foot of the mountain scattered; they were
        frightened.
    Q'aq'awitz tarried in the mountain.
    They let fall his destiny; it died in their hearts.
    Perhaps he would bring fire.
    Perhaps he would not bring it to them.
    Many sparks fell to the foot of the mountain.
    They hit some [people], they didn't hit others.

Figure 4.3 This image from the CZ–N (Nuttall [1902] 1975, page 13) depicts a volcano, denoted by the lava (painted red in the codex) spewing from its peak. The human figure suggests how an individual entering or exiting a volcano might have been portrayed as a prompt for the following *.öq* subheading. Three or four additional images would have been used for the subsequent four subheadings.

Reproduced courtesy of Dover Publications, New York.

Then (,öq) he came out of the mountain.

    In truth his face was frightening when he came out of the mountain, Q'aq'xanul.

    All the warriors, the Seven Amaq's said: "In truth, his divining power, his nawal,

        His power and his majesty are frightening.

    It [the fire] died, it has descended," they said.

    Immediately, then (öq) he was seated on his chair.

Then (,öq) he came down.

    In truth, they honored him.

    All of them said: *"You, our younger brother, you brought down the fire of the mountain.*

You passed the fire down.

You, our hair; you our heads," said all the warriors, the Seven Amaq's to Q'aq'awitz.

Then (,öq) he said to them:

    "The heart of the mountain, my captive, my prisoner has come, you, my younger brothers, my older brothers."

Then (,öq) the heart of the mountain was unwrapped.

    Fire was balled up as a stone.

    This stone was named Saqchoq' [white flint]; it was not green-stone.

    There were thirteen masks with the stone.

    This is the Xtz'ul dance; the heart of the mountain, Q'aq'xanul.

    It is said that the dancing of the Xtz'ul is difficult.

    Many divisions performed it; their ornaments were innumerable.

¶ They came there again.

    They passed through the place known as Sesïk Inup [Floating Ceiba]

    It was just floating on the lake.

    The ceiba was not planted.

    The ceiba had no roots; it just bobbed on the water.

That is why it is named Sesïk Inup.

They passed over the hill known as K'alala' Pakay [Tied Pacaya].

The pacaya leaves were tied in bundles and used as seats.

This it was named K'alala' Pakay, say our grandfathers.

Excerpt is taken from Maxwell and Hill (2006, 91–112).

The Bringing of the Iqomaq's [Presented] Here

¶ Then (Öq) those called Kaqixajay and K'ub'ulajay were seen from afar; they were the vassals of the Iqomaq's.

They were brought, driven by them.

Later the hill named Chi Q'alib'al [At the Reclining Place] was found.

They gave themselves up; pitiful them!

Then (,öq) it was found.

They reclined themselves.

Thus the mountain was named Chi Q'alib'al.

They said when (öq) they gave themselves up: *"I am just your younger brother, your older brother.*

I was defeated, I will carry your throne, your chair.

I am also a winäq; I have my vassals," said the Iqomaq's.

The Kaqixajay and the K'ub'ulajay were their vassals.

Thus was the bringing of the Iqomaq'.

And just so were they saved.

They engendered the Sotz'il people; the fathers, the grandfathers of the Ajpo Sotz'il.

K'ulawi' Sochoj and K'ulawi' K'anti' were their names.

Their vassals left, they no longer had vassals.

¶ Then (Öq) they arrived atop the hill of K'aqb'atz'ulu'.

Then (,öq) the one named Tolk'om was found.

It was truly frightening; the hill, K'aqb'atz'ulu', was shaking.

First all the warriors finished arriving.

They were frightened.

They had not yet begun the killing.

Then (,töq) he [Q'aq'awitz] arrived.

>All the warriors said: *"You have finally arrived, you our younger brother.*
>
>*What is this? It is in truth frightening!"* they said.
>
>Our grandfather Q'aq'awitz said:
>
>>*"Who is it then, you warriors? So we will go see his face. He is not our enemy.*
>>
>>*We shall not use arrows [and] shields."*
>
>*"You are there, you, our elder brothers,"* they said.
>
>All of them were sent to capture Tolk'om

Then (,öq) they said: *"What can be done, you, our younger brother?*

>*We tried it; in truth it was frightening there.*
>
>*You go there of your own free will,"* said all of them.

Then (,töq) he [Q'aq'awitz] went to see Tolk'om; he arrived.

>It was truly frightening there; the hill shook.
>
>He said to Tolk'om: *"Who are you? You are not my younger brother, my older brother.*
>
>>*You are you? Now I will kill you!"*
>
>Immediately he [Tolk'om] was frightened. *He said: "I am the child of mud, of muck.*
>
>>*This is just my house where I am, you, lord,"* he said.
>
>*"Pay [tribute] now! Do not move!"* he said to Tolk'om.

Then (,öq) he gave himself up, he was taken.

>He [Q'aq'awitz] came back, having captured him.
>
>He arrived back with them.
>
>It was said [by Q'aq'awitz] to the warriors, the Seven Amaq's when (öq) Tolk'om gave himself up:

"We will glorify this hill.

You [will] inaugurate, my war-prisoner, my captive.

We will propitiate it, we will sacrifice the head of my war-prisoner.

We will adorn him, just shoot him.

We will glorify its name.

This hill called K'aqb'atz'ulu' by the original people, you, lords,"
was said to all the warriors.

¶ Thus they said this:

"You are our younger brother.

One is the first child, another is the last born of ours.

We will measure the day, the light, in council.

We, the thirteen divisions of warriors will provide your canopy,
your bench, your chair, your lordship."

They, two of the children [of the] Sotz'il [and] Tukuche' are told:

"You will descend among the Ajpo Sotz'il [and] Ajpo Xajil.

You are instructed.

Just there do it.

Even if you are one kind of warriors, nonetheless there are you
younger brothers, your older brothers: they are the B'akaj Poq',
the B'akaj Xajil."

Nevertheless they are told: The power and majesty are alike, you,
our younger brother!" it was said.

Then (,Tōq) his supplicatory offering was given him.

Then (,öq) the Ajpo Sotz'il [and] Ajpo Xajil gave himself up.

"Even though we are the Sotz'il [and] Tuquche', nonetheless those
are our younger brothers, our older brothers; those, the B'akaj
Poqoj, we, the B'akaj Xajil, you, our sons!" said our ancient
fathers and grandfathers.

"We are a different sort of warrior," just because great was their
divining power, their transforming power.

And they were bearers of the arrows, the shields.

Thus they, our first fathers were given as supplicatory offerings to them.

Therefore, they greatly abased the day [fortune] of their birth.

Figure 4.4 This climactic scene from the CZ–N (Nuttall [1902] 1975, page 84) depicts a specific example of the widespread Mesoamerican Arrow Sacrifice, analogous to the one described in the following three *Small subheadings*, though here the victim is tied to a scaffold rather than a tree. The quantity of imagery in the scene, such as additional personages, would probably have been much greater so as to convey all of the action in the following *Small subheading with serif* and two *,öq* subheadings.

Reproduced courtesy of Dover Publications, New York.

¶ Then (Öq) began the killing of Tolk'om
  First he was bedecked, first he was adorned.
  Immediately his arms were stretched out upon the *lama'* tree.
  There he was shot.

Then (,öq) began the dancing by all the warriors, so "Tolk'om" the song was named.

They danced.

Then (,öq) his shooting began.
  What came from the strings of their bows were not arrows.
  They were long wooden spears with which he was shot.
  On the mountain of K'aqb'atz'ulu' they were shot.
  First went all their arrows.
  And then (öq) went the arrow of our grandfather, Q'aq'awitz.
  Quickly it passed to the hill.
  The [arrow] was named Che' Tz'ulu'.
  With it, he shot Tolk'om.
  It was this [arrow] that killed [him].
  And then (öq) all the warriors [shot].
  Few of their arrows went in.
  From afar they shot them.
  Thus, then (öq) the person died.
  Lots of blood came out on the bark of the *lama'* tree when (öq)
      he was cut to pieces.
  He was presented before the Seven Amaq's [and] all the warriors.
  He was dismembered; he was sacrificed.
  His death was when [the month of] Uchum was celebrated.
  "Let it come to pass each year that food and drink be prepared;
      that children shoot arrows with the tunay [tree] as his substitute.
  Let them shoot as if it were Tolk'om!" said our grandfathers of
      yore, you, our sons!
  Thus we brought him there with the Sotz'il and the Tuquche'.
  Because of his [Tolk'om's] divining power, his transforming
      power, his glory, his majesty, he was promised as a sacrifice
      there.
  As for our fathers, our grandfathers, of us the Kaqchikel winäq,
      the day [fortune] of their birth was not defeated, they our
      ancient grandfathers.

¶ Then (Öq) they came from there on the hill K'aqb'atz'ulu'.

They cast pieces of Tolk'om into the lake.

Then (,öq) it became famous as "Tolk'om's Casting Point."

Figure 4.5 This image from the CZ–N (Nuttal [1902] 1975, page 75) suggests how people crossing a body of water in boats might have been depicted as a prompt for the following two *,öq Small subheadings*. The third subheading below illustrates how much dialog—which could not be portrayed pictographically—an indigenous historian would need to have memorized.

Reproduced courtesy of Dover Publications, New York.

Then (,öq) they said: *"Let us pass through the lake."*
    Just a few had crossed, when everyone became frightened, when
        (öq) they [Tolk'om's pieces] stirred the lake.
    Where they were cast is named Pan Pati', Pa Yan Ch'oköl.
    The signs of their transforms emerged there; this was at Chi
        Tulul.

Then (,öq) all the warriors began to cross the lake.

After them went Q'aq'awitz.

He had a sister named Chetejaw.

She remained where they cast them [the pieces of Tolk'om].

This is the point named K'ab'owil Ab'äj.

Now, then (töq) Q'aq'awitz went.

It was frightening when (öq) he went into the water.

He turned into a cloud-snake.

Immediately, the waves became dark.

The wind, the red whirlwind arose over the water.

The stirring inside the lake ceased.

He [Q'aq'awitz] wanted something; he wanted the day [fortune]
    of the Tz'utujils brought down.

He saw all the Seven Amaq's.

Then (,öq) they emerged from the water.

They were there.

He said to those who engendered the Tz'ikinajay:

*"Just now we stirred the depth of our lake, our ocean, you, our
    older brother.*

One part is your lake; one part for your tasty things: your ducks,
your crabs, your fish,"

they were told.

He [the Tz'ikinajay leader] replied: *"Fine, you, my younger brother.*

Another part is your lake, another [part] for your tasty things: your
    ducks, your crabs, your fish.

Another [part] is for your reeds, your green cane.

But there is this, just after you set the people, someone was killing
    in Chachux,"

said the Aj Tz'ikinajay to him [Q'aq'awitz].

They came again; they split up.

But he returned there.

He wanted to cross [the lake] and bring his sister.

He had not yet brought her because of the Nik'aj Ko'on.

His sister did not appear again; he no longer sensed her.

He said: *"Where did my sister go? Who took her?*

In truth, I am going to look for her; I will find her yet," he said.

His heart turned to war again.

They [the warriors] bedecked themselves.

In truth, it was frightening when (öq) they went to look for his sister.

Immediately, the Tz'utujil Amaq' became frightened.

He [Q'aq'awitz] said when he arrived: *"Who took my sister?*

My heart is again in the mood for war!" he said this to the amaq's:
    Tz'utujils, Ko'ons, [and] Tz'ununs.

Immediately, the Aj Tz'ikinajay argued with him: *"You, lord; you are*
    my younger brother, my elder brother.

but your sister is accustomed to this place.

We just divided our lake; one part is your lake, one part is my lake,"
    he said.

His warriors when the Aj Tz'ikinajay surrendered.

Our grandfather Q'aq'awitz said next: *"Why do they bring forth my*
    sister?

Well, thus she will remain with the Nik'aj Ko'on.

I will just heed your words, you, my younger brother.

Let the Nik'aj Ko'on defeat me.

There is nothing I will do to him," he said then, *"They are just*
    Tz'ikinajays."

Thus was the division of this lake, said our grandfathers.

And thus, we and the Tz'utujils are related as younger brothers, as
    older brothers.

There is more [of this story] that we will not enter.

There they crossed; thence they returned quickly, our first grandfa-
    thers, Q'aq'awitz [and] Saktekaw.

It was in darkness, it was at night when (,öq) they did this.

It had not yet (öq) dawned, they say.

It was just a little while before it dawned there.

They arrived, thus, on the hill Pulch'ich'.

From there they were sent out.

5

Res Gestae Accounts and Genealogy:
The Twins and Their Descendants

THE CONTENT OF THE NEXT SECTIONS of the Xajil Chronicle conforms better with a res gestae format than with a cartographic one. It begins with the story of Q'aq'awitz's twin sons, Ka'i' No'j and Ka'i' B'atz'. In these episodes, movement from place to place is decidedly subordinate to interactions in situ among a small group of characters. The twins present themselves before Tepew. They converse briefly. Place is not specified. They are commissioned by Tepew to collect tribute. They receive gold bindings on their bachelor's topknots. They go to the lord of the Tz'kinajay but their journey there is not described. Unlike cartographic histories, they do not pass over named topographical features like hills, rivers, or lakes. Given that the Tz'ikinajay lived on the shore of Lake Atitlan, the fact that the account does not refer to it would seem to be a significant omission for a cartographic account.

The Twins' topknots are cut off while they sleep by the daughters of the Tz'ikinajay lords. These women are named, as are their fathers. The Twins are afraid that they have disgraced themselves and that Tepew will be angry. They hide in a cave but there is no account of a journey to get there. In the event, the cave is named only subsequently as "Ka'i' No'j's Cave." They are found, but there is no account of the places the searchers looked for them. Again, this is a very different form of account and continues down to the Tuquche' revolt.

Excerpt taken from Maxwell and Hill (2006, 134–146)

Here their Journey [the Twins Ka'i' Noj and Ka'i' B'atz] to Tepew

Figure 5.1 This image from the CZ–N (Nuttall [1902] 1975, page 10) is used to suggest how the Twins' audience with Tepew might have been portrayed as a prompt for the following *Small subheading with serif*. Two additional images would have been used to complete this brief section of the account.

Reproduced courtesy of Dover Publications, New York.

¶ Our grandfathers Ka'i' Noj [and] Ka'i' B'atz went to Tepew.

　　They went alone; they just remained alone, the Q'alel Xajil [and] the Ajuchan Xajil.

　　They arrived before Tepew.

　　"Who are you?" They were asked by Tepew.

　　"We are the sons of Q'aq'awitz," this they said, Ka'i' Noj [and] Ka'i' B'atz.

　　Tepew was astonished when [öq] he heard their words.

　　Thus they were elevated [in rank] by Tepew.

　　They had been humble when they went to him.

¶ Then (Töq) they were sent by Tepew to bring tribute.

They went to bring tribute of the amaq's.

They were no longer humble, rather [they were] over the amaq' for the bringing of tribute.

Truly, everyone was frightened at the divining power, the transforming power of Ka'i' Noj [and Ka'i' B'atz].

They were burning at night like fire.

They were shaking too, like the earthquake.

Thus, the amaq' was frightened.

Then (,öq) they came to power over the amaq's.

Everything was given to them by the amaq's, their bringing of tribute.

There in the east, their topknots were adorned with precious metal.

Precious metal was the binding of their topknots.

The tribute was brought by the amaq's.

Their words were obeyed.

Thus they were made sons of Tepew for what happened, for what they did.

In truth they were loved [by Tepew] because of it.

Here the Giving of their Wives

¶ They went, they the tribute collectors, to those of Tz'ikinajay

Our grandfathers outgrew their youth.

There among the Tz'ikinajay they were given their wives.

But their topknots were coveted,

Their topknots wrapped with precious metal.

Then (,öq) they arrived.

Those of Tz'ikinajay said: *"Let us make Tepew's messengers our sons-in-law!"*

"Truly, their transforming power is frightening!"

"Let us give them wives!"

"Let us take their topknots!"

But the words of the [Tz'ikinajay] lords did not reach Ka'i' Noj
    and Ka'i' B'atz.

They [the lords] were frightened, they [the twins] had power,
    they felt.

Their topknots were stolen at night by the daughters of the lords.

Their topknots were stealthily cut off while they slept.

It was the daughters of lords Jun Sunk'un Q'anel May Ajaw
    [and] Pusi Ajaw who Ka'i' Noj [and] Ka'i' B'atz married.

Here are the names of their wives: B'ub'atz'o was one's name;

Ikxiw was the name of the other.

Our grandfathers no longer felt their topknots; they were afraid.

This they said: *"Do not disgrace us, you of Tz'ikinajay! Tepew
    will be angry with us!"*

They said: *"Do not be frightened! We will give you wives.*

We will make you our sons-in-law.

We will not do any more evil.

Go, so that it may be told to Tepew through you," they were told.

Figure 5.2 Though part of a place-name in the CZ–N (Nuttall [1902 1975, page 61),
the image is used here to suggest how an individual hiding in a cave might have
appeared as a prompt for the following *,Tōq subheading*. Two images probably were
used to convey the two preceding *Small subheadings*.

Reproduced courtesy of Dover Publications, New York.

Then (,Töq) their wives were given to them.
 They went so it would be told to Tepew.
 But they did not go there.
 They were fearful of Tepew.
 Immediately, they hid in a cave.
 They stayed hidden for a long time in a cave.
 This cave was named Pa Rupek Ka'i' Noj, it is said.

Figure 5.3   This CZ–N image (Nuttall [1902] 1975, page 45) portrays a conversation between two individuals, with the figure on the right sitting in a cave. Note the speech-scroll emerging from the mouth of the figure on the left. Something similar might have been used as the prompt for the entirety of the following *Large subheading with Wa'e'*.

Reproduced courtesy of Dover Publications, New York.

Here the Search for Them

¶ (Töq) Then they were sought by the chinamïts

"Let us go look for our ajpops, wherever they may be!

We disgraced ourselves, we heard their words.

But they are not serving as their mothers [and] fathers,"

This said the Q'eqak'ak'üch, B'ak'ajol, Kaweq [and] Sib'aqijay to
    Ka'i' Noj [and] Ka'i' B'atz.

Then (,töq) they were found in the cave.

Those who were searching for them said when they arrived:

"We were looking for you, you our ajpops.

In truth, we are pitiful," they said.

Immediately, Ka'i' Noj [and] Ka'i' B'atz said: *"Let us not go.*

Don't you have your lords Q'alel [and] Ajuchan?

What does Tepew want with us?

Did we not humbly go to Tepew?

Let us not go, unless they [the usurpers] die, those whose words
    you obeyed.

Let us go that it be straightened out with Tepew!

Let us go immediately!" they said.

Immediately, the chinamïts obeyed.

Immediately, a messenger, a negotiator, went to Tepew.

Immediately, Tepew was happy when he heard their news.

And they, too, were happy: the Kaqchikel, Sotz'il [and] Tuquche'

Those of Tz'ikinajay were also happy when our grandfathers
    were found.

Here their Return to Pan Che', Chi Q'ojom

¶ They arrived there accompanied by their wives.

Thus their faces were seen again.

All the amaq's were happy when they arrived.

Immediately, they were hanged; they died: the Q'alel Xajil, the
    Ajuchan Xajil, and all their descendants then died.

¶ They entered lordship.

Ka'i' Noj became Ajpop Xajil.

Ka'i' B'atz became Ajpop K'amajay

The two of them became lords.

Here is the set of descendants when they entered lordship.

¶ They begat sons and daughters, Ka'i' Noj [and Ka'i' B'atz].

One of them begat four sons.

The other begat five sons.

They were nine males whom Ka'i' Noj and Ka'i' B'atz begat.

Just these were their descendants.

It was frightening the divining power, the transforming power of
    Q'aq'awitz [and] Saktqkaw, [of] Ka'i' Noj [and] Ka'i' B'atz.

¶ Then (Öq) Ka'i' Noj [and] Ka'i' B'atz said:

"Let us complete our lordship as our grandfathers counseled us!

Let two of our sons enter lordship!" they said.

Then (,töq), one of the sons of Ka'i' Noj entered the office of Aju-
    chan Xajil.

Likewise, a son of Ka'i' B'atz entered the office of Q'alel Xajil.

Thus we had four lords, we Xajils.

The lordship of our grandfathers was complete among them.

Genealogical Passages

Like the Nahua-speakers but in contrast with the Mixtecs, the Kaqchikel
understood themselves to be migrants and recent arrivals in their home
territory. The Mixtecs believed they had been created in situ. Their
genealogies are deep. These genealogies include both sons and daughters, as well as their eventual spouses, thereby tracking the complex
dynastic relationships among the many small polities of the region. In
contrast, most of the Kaqchikel migration was under the leadership of
the semilegendary Q'aq'awitz. From him, there are only eight genera-

tions of rulers down to the Spanish conquest in 1524 and, without calendrical dates in the accounts, we cannot gauge the length of their respective reigns (see Wauchope 1949 for an attempt to do so).

Despite these differences, the presentation of genealogies in the alphabetic text of the Xajil Chronicle parallels the pictographic presentation in Mixtec codices such as the Codex Zouche–Nuttall. First, in both accounts the presentation is generational; there is no summary presentation of an entire line of descent. Second, offspring are listed immediately after their parents' marriage, with birth order inferred by placement in pictographic examples. Third, the focus of both kinds of narratives is on the career of the heir to lordship. Fourth, other descendants' marriages are not recorded, nor are they even mentioned again unless they succeed to lordship, or, in the case of males, are killed in battle, or sacrificed after being taken prisoner in battle. For a concrete example, see the text that follows.

Excerpt from Maxwell and Hill (2006, 191–197).

Figure 5.4 Deceased lords in the CZ–N are typically depicted wrapped in funeral bundles. Here (Nuttall [1902] 1975, page 20) the pair of them suggest the prompt for the *Small subheading with serif* below.

The Death of the Lords [presented] Here

(genealogy within res gestae format)

¶ The lord Jun Toj was the first to die.

Then (,öq), died also the lord Wuqu' B'atz'.

The town was already completed when the lords died.

¶ Then (Töq) another became lord, Lajuj Aj was his name, the first son of the lord Jun Toj.

Figure 5.5 Though not part of a genealogical passage, this image from the CZ–N (Nuttall [1902] 1975, page 20) suggests how the fact of descendants' deaths in battle might have been portrayed in the *Small subheading with seriph* below. Four additional images probably would have been used in the subsequent section, beginning with another *Small subheading with serif*.

Reproduced courtesy of Dover Publications, New York.

¶ Then (Töq) another became lord, Oxlajuj Tz'i' was his name, the
　　first son of the lord Wuqu' B'atz'.

The lord, our grandfather, begat nine males.

Sib'aqijay Ximox was the name of the wife of lord Wuqu' B'atz'.

Oxlajuj Tz'i' was the name of the first son;

Lord Kab'lajuj B'atz' was the name of the second;

Chopena' Tojin was the name of the third;

Chopena' Tz'ikin Uk'a' was the name of the fourth.

These two of our grandfathers fell in war.

Chopena' Tojin went and fell.

Tukuru' Kaqixala' was the name of the hill where he fell.

Chopena' Tz'ikin Uk'a fell at Atakat.

Chopena' Kej was the name of the fifth;

Nima Ajin, the sixth

Just Ajin was the name of the seventh;

Kawoq [and] K'atu' were the names of the other two.

All these grandfathers of ours were powerful warriors.

¶ And so our grandfather, Oxlajuj Tz'i' as well as Lajuj Aj were in
　　truth awesome warriors.

Their knowledge, too, was awesome.

They did not forget the words of their fathers, their grandfathers.

The hearts of the vassals were contented when they entered
　　lordship.

Thus the lords again exerted power and majesty.

And they waged many wars.

Lord Lajuj Aj also died.

Then (,öq), entered lordship the lord named Kab'lajuj Tijax, the
　　first son of the lord Lajuj Aj.

It was lord Oxlajuj Tz'i' who was ruling when Kab'lajuj Tijax
　　also became lord.

So it was that the lords were and remained powerful.

In truth, upon the death of K'iqab', the nawal lord there at
　　K'iche', then the K'iche'

Winäq again waged war against the Kaqchikel Winäq.

Those ruling K'iche' at the time were named Tepepul [and]
Istayul.

Then (, töq), the hearts of the K'iche' Winäq turned hateful toward
the town at Iximche'.

In truth, there was a great famine when fell a great frost that
killed the cornfields in

[the month of] Uchum.

The cornfields were destroyed by the cold.

Thus provisions were distributed, said your grandfathers, you,
my sons.

Then (.öq) he brought down [the news] to the K'iche' Winäq.

Just one man, a runner, left the Kaqchikel.

He arrived among the K'iche',

bringing news of the famine to K'iche'.

The man said this: *"In truth, there is great famine,*

the people have no more strength due to the famine."

He said this when he arrived among the K'iche'.

Thus was assured the killing of the Kaqchikel by the K'iche'
Winäq, death in their hearts.

6

Annals History

THE ANNALS SECTION OF THE Chronicle begins with the Tuquche' revolt as its starting point. *Large subheadings* set off each year and serifs set off each event therein. The length of entries varies widely. In some years nothing noteworthy occurred and we see similar "empty" years in the Mexican annals histories, such as the Codex Aubin (see Figure 6.1). The Xajil Chronicle now exhibits a concern with time that equals its Mexican counterparts. In addition to noting the day of the year on which fell the anniversary of the Tuquche' revolt, day names are also used for the specific events that occurred during that year.

Figure 6.1 Examples from the Codex Aubin simplified here to show only the essentials of the account's structure. This image from the much longer annals account depicts the years from 1541 (*top*) to 1545 (*bottom*). Note that nothing of sufficient importance to be recorded occurred in 1544, in contrast to the other years. This absence of events for a specific year is reflected in the alphabetic text of the annals portion of the Xajil Chronicle.

Excerpts are taken from Maxwell and Hill (2006, 228–237).

On Eight Aj Fell the Anniversary of the Revolt

On Five Aj Ended the Second Year since the Revolt

On Two Aj Ended the Third Year since the Revolt

¶ It was on three Kej that another revolt occurred, among the K'iche'.
    It came to pass, as it had with the Tuquche' revolt, there among
        the K'iche'

On Twelve Aj Ended the Fourth Year since the Revolt

¶ In the fifth year also died those of Mixku', the sustainers of lord
    Kab'lajuj Tijax.
    They were about to exalt themselves.
    On seven Kamey the town of Mixku' fell.
    They were dissolved unto death by the warriors.
¶ Then (Öq) the Yaki', those of Xiwiku, died.
    The lord of the Aqajal Winäq was the ally of the lord Wo'o
        Kawoq when (öq) they raised themselves up on the mountain.
    The Aqajal Winäq were about to become powerful again there.

¶ [It was] six days from the fifth anniversary of the revolt.

Then (,öq) the Aqajal Winäq died on the mountain.
    The lord Wo'o' Kawoq was about to become great again on
        the mountain.

On Nine Aj Ended the Fifth Year since the Revolt

On Six Aj Ended the Sixth Year since the Revolt

On Three Aj Ended the Seventh Year since the Revolt

¶ In the eighth year [since] the revolt, the Tz'utujils died again because of those of Xe' Inup.

At Xepalika' they were dissolved unto death.

Saqb'in Ajmaq fell on thirteen Ajmaq.

On Thirteen Aj Ended the Eighth Year since the Revolt

On Eleven Aj Ended the Thirteenth Year since the Revolt

¶ On thirteen Tz'ikin, Xoq'ojaw Wo'o Kej died; the wife of Lajuj Tijax, the son of K'iqab'.

Just a little was lacking for the completion of the fourteenth year since the revolt when lord Oxlajuj Tz'i', our grandfather, died.

On three Ajmaq the lord died.

Truly, his power as a lord was awesome.

The day of his birth was unbeaten.

He waged many wars, he conquered many towns before he died

These are the sons the lord sired:

¶ Jun Iq' was the name of the first son.

He was the one who entered into lordship when the lord Oxlajuj Tz'i', his father, died.

All four of the amaq's [pledged their] word when Jun Iq' assumed lordship.

Waqaqi' Ajmaq was the name of the second child.

Noj was the third child.

B'eleje' K'at was the fourth child.

Imox was the fifth child.

Noj was the sixth child.

Maqu' Xq'ujay was the name of the Xoq'ojaw, the wife of the lord Oxlajuj Tz'i'.

7

Cartographic Accounts of Battle

S OME BATTLE ACCOUNTS SEEM TOO detailed to have been conveyed as simple entries in an annals format or as small loci in a large cartographic history. One way to deal with such complex events would have been to create a separate, ancillary cartographic document to provide the necessary degree of detail. Such documents could be created to record recent events and become part of a polity's historical collection. Thus, the writing of history was an ongoing process, not just the rememberance of events of the distant past. Brief but unequivocal evidence for the creation of such documents appears in multiple entries in Bernal Díaz del Castillo's account:

> They [the Tlaxcallans] brought us *pictures of the battles they had fought* with the Mexicans painted on large henequen cloths, showing their manner of fighting. (Díaz del Castillo 1956, 157)

Commenting on the battle against the Aztecs of Tenochtitlan by the Spanish and their Tlaxcallan allies he states:

> Many times I have seen among the Mexicans and Tlaxcalans, *paintings of this battle*, and the ascent we made of the great Cue [pyramid], as they look upon it as a very heroic deed. And although in the pictures they have made of it, they depict all of us badly wounded and streaming with blood and many of us dead, this setting fire to the Cue, when so many warriors were guarding it in both the battlements and recesses, and many more Indians were below on the ground and the courts were full of them and there were many more on the sides; and with our [siege] towers destroyed, how was it possible to scale it? (Díaz del Castillo 1956, 308)

He also indicates that accounts could be painted "as needed" to convey to the Aztec ruler the latest intelligence concerning the Spaniards' arrival and progress; effectively a means of recording "current events." In an interview with Cortés, Díaz del Castillo quotes Moctezuma as stating that he had received prior news of the Spaniards' arrival through "pictures" of the battles they had already fought:

> That it must indeed be true that we were those of whom his ancestors in years long past had spoken, saying that men would come from where the sun rose to rule over these lands, and that we must be those men, as we had fought so

valiantly in the affairs at Champoton and Tabasco and against the Tlaxcalans: *for they had brought him pictures of the battles true to life.* (Díaz del Castillo 1956, 204)

In a later interview he again quotes Moctezuma informing Cortés:

Only now messengers have come to tell me that at the port where you landed there have arrived eighteen more ships and many people and horses, and they have brought it all to me *painted on some cloths.* (Díaz del Castillo 1956, 258)

The Historia Tolteca–Chichimeca contains a detailed battle scene similar to the ones described by Díaz del Castillo and that suggests how such an event might have been rendered in the Xajil Chronicle. The scene was painted in the mid-sixteenth century, some three decades after the Spanish conquest (Leibsohn 2006; Kirchhoff, Odena Güemes, Reyes García 1976). The battle it depicts occurred in preconquest times, however. Painted on adjoining pages in a European-influenced style and in book format, the scene occupies an area of 27 by 38.5 cm. This is a significant amount of space for a single event, far more space than could have been devoted to a single incident in even a large cartographic history (compare with battle scenes in the Lienzo de Quauhquechollan, see, p. 96). It also represents a considerable amount of effort that, likewise, likely would have been prohibitive in a large cartographic history.

The two most elaborate accounts of battle in the Xajil Chronicle concern a fight against the K'iche' and the Tuquche' revolt. The K'iche' battle is dealt with under two *Large subheadings with Wa'e'*, which in this case likely represent two sections of a single cartographic document. In both accounts, the battles are joined initially at specific locations. There are multiple units of troops and flanking moves from specific starting points. Roads and a "bridge" are mentioned. Commanders and prominent enemy casualties and prisoners are named. Four women-warriors participate in the Tuquche' action and presumably all of the action and characters could only have been represented in a document analogous to the Historia Tolteca–Chichimeca presented in Figure 7.1.

Excerpt from Maxwell and Hill (2006, 197–204).

Figure 7.1 Though not in the Mixteca–Puebla style, this elaborate battle scene from the mid-sixteenth-century Historia Tolteca–Chichimeca (Kirchhoff et al. 1976) suggests how an extended account of a battle might have been portrayed. In this format there is adequate space in which individual figures, representing either specific heroes or entire detachments of troops, can be portrayed, along with topographic features. A scene like this might have been adequate to prompt the content of the following two *Large subheadings with Wa'e'* or the subsequent Death of the Tuquche' account.

Reproduced courtesy of the Instituto Nacional de Antropología e Historia.

Their Arrival [presented] Here

¶ Then [Töq] [the K'iche' army] came, it wrested itself from the town
    of Q'umarkaaj.

    After all the lords had come forth, came their god-image, Tojojil.

    The warriors came from everywhere, innumerable people.

    Not just 8000 nor 16000 came, they arrived from all the amaq's.

    They arrived there and donned feathers.

    The arrived and counseled there.

Then (,öq) they bedecked themselves with bows, with shields,
     with spears,
          with quetzal battle-plumes, with battle armor [and] with crowns
               of precious metal [and] gems.
     Thus adorned, they came forth.

¶ It was on ten Tz'i', the concerted descent of the K'iche' Winäq
     on Iximche'
          Our grandfathers, Oxlajuj Tz'i' [and] Kab'lajuj Tijax, had not
               yet heard the news when the K'iche' Winäq arrived here;
                    killers of the Sotz'il [and] Tuquche'.
          Suddenly, a runner brought down news of the [impending] death
               to the lords.
          *"In two days there will be death, when all the K'iche' Winäq have
               come; killers of the people.*
          The town will be invaded.
          *Truly, it is frightening how they came, not just 8000 nor 16000
               warriors!"* said the runner when he reached the
                    Kaqchikels.
          Immediately, the lords held council.
          They said: *"It has been heard. It is good that it [the news] has come.*
          We will test ourselves with the K'iche' Winäq," said the lords.
          Immediately, a leader went out.
          One division of warriors went out to cut off the K'iche' Winäq.
          They were cut off.
          Only those of the town confronted them.
          They descended upon the great road above the hill, K'atb'e Yaki.
          They confronted the enemy, those of Tib'ak'oy, those of Raxaqän,
               those of Q'ale'aj, those of Pa Saqi'ulew [and] those of
                    Q'inon closed their path.

¶ Then (Töq) the warriors adorned themselves with bows, with
     shields, with spears.
          They [Iximche' warriors] were already waiting when they [K'iche'
               warriors] descended.

The Death of the K'iche' Winäq' [presented] Here

In truth, when dawn broke over the earth, they [the K'iche']
descended from the top of the hill.
Immediately, shouts and battle-cries blossomed.
Immediately, the flag was raised.
Flutes, war-drums, [and] conch trumpets resounded.
In truth, it was frightening when the K'iche' Winäq descended.
Early, they fell into deadfalls, which had already been covered
over.
They descended to the foot of the hill.
In truth, they arrived beside the Selejay Ya'
The lords Tepepul [and] Istayul came forth as commanders,
accompanied hither by their god-image.

Then (Töq) the ambushers came out from behind [the K'iche'].
In truth, it was frightening when they came.
Immediately resounded shouts [and] war-cries, flutes, war
drums, [and] conch trumpets.
The warriors demonstrated their divining power, their trans-
forming power.
Immediately, the K'iche' Winäq paled, they fought no more.
Immediately, they were shattered.
The K'iche' Winäq were dissolved into death; countless died.
And those who survived were enslaved.
The lords Tepepul [and] Istayul gave themselves up.
Their god-image gave himself up.
In this way the Ruq'alel Achi', the Rajpop Achi', the grandson
[and] the son of the lord, [the] Ajxit, [the] Ajpwäq, [the]
Ajtz'ib'. [and the] Ajk'ot, [and] all of the warriors were,
in truth, dissolved into death.
Countless, not just 8000, nor 16000 of the K'iche' Winäq were
killed by the Kaqchikel long ago, said our fathers, our
grandfathers, you, my sons!

It was lord Oxlajuj Tz'i', Kab'lajuj Tijax, lord W'o'o Imox [and]
    Roqel B'atzin who did it.
Never before had the hill of Iximche' become so mighty!

Excerpt is taken from Maxwell and Hill (2006, 220–225).

The Death of the Tuquche' [presented] Here
Truly, They Were Dissolved into Death

¶ When the day broke on eleven Aj, the Tuquche' burst forth from
    the other town.
    Immediately resounded the flutes [and] war drums of lord
        Ka'i' Junajpu'.
    He was adorned with arms, with quetzal war-plumes, with war
        armor, with a crown of gold, [and] jems.

Then (,öq) they burst out from Ch'aqaya'.
    They were truly frightening.
    Innumerable were the Tuquche'.
    There were not just 8000, nor 16000.

Then (,Töq) the fighting began before the town.
    The battle was joined at the foot of the bridge.
    Chukuy B'atz'in was the leader [against] the revolt by the
        Tuquche'.
    Four women were bedecked with cotton armor.
    The warriors gave them [the women] their war bows.
    Likewise, each of the four women was given their arrows, before
        the mat of Chukuy B'atz'in.
    Frightening was the great revolt which the lords made long ago.
    To the leader of the fighting the women exhibited their flesh,
        before the edifice of the lords of the Sotz'il [and] the Xajil.
    The women went out from there.

Indeed, they went out first from that place when a division of
    troops burst out on the great road at Nimak'otoj.
They were solely the warriors of those of Tib'ak'oy [and] those
    of Raxaqän.
Early they broke out on the great road.
Only two fell when they broke out.
The Tuquche' descended from the other town.
The fighting lasted a long time.
The Rajpop Achi', Sinajitoj, of Xe chi Peqen, cut [them] off.

¶ Then (Töq) the flanker came up behind the Tukuche'.
Immediately, they fought no more.
They were soon shattered.
The warriors were dissolved, the women [and] children were
    dissolved, into death.
The lord Ka'i' Junajpu' gave himself up.
The lords Tz'irin Iyu' Toxk'om Noj [and] all the grandsons [and]
    sons of the lord gave themselves up.
Immediately, those of Tib'ak'oy [and] those of Raxaqän went to
    the K'iche'.
Others went to the Tz'utujils.
All of the vassals offered themselves as client outsiders
    [elsewhere].
They were all shattered.
Thus were the Tuquche' dissolved long ago, you, my sons!
It was our grandfathers, Oxlajuj Tz'i' [and] Kab'lajuj Tijax who
    did this.
On eleven Aj it was done; the Tuquche' were shattered.

A Cartographic Account of the Spanish Conquest?

After a normal entry noting the completion of the twenty-eighth anniversary of the Tuquche' revolt, a new *Large subheading with Wa'e* begins
the conquest account. An additional five such subheadings structure

the account down through 1527. As noted earlier, these subheadings
seem to indicate either major divisions of a cartographic history or a
switch from one document to another. In this instance, I believe there
was a switch from the pictographic annals to a cartographic format.
"Day" dates remain significant information in this section but they could
easily have been placed within the cartographic format, as sometimes
occurred in central Mexican practice.

The account of the Spanish entry into the Maya highlands and the
subsequent campaigns and sufferings of the Kaqchikel contains many
more dates and measures of time than any other portion of the annals
section. But movement to named places is equally prominent, though
details of the actions performed in these places are rudimentary. The
Spanish suddenly arrive at Xe Tulul. Their leader is Tunatiw (Alvarado).
There is a battle at Xe Tulul on the day 1 Q'anel and the K'iche' are
defeated. The Spanish proceed to Xelajub', where they again defeat the
K'iche'. Alvarado and his army arrive at the K'iche' capital, Q'umarkaaj,
where he is greeted by the lords, whom he immediately shackles. On
4 K'at the K'iche' lords are burned on Alvarado's order. The Spanish
army arrives at Iximche' on 1 Junajpu'. Five days later they leave to
defeat the Tz'utujils, which occurs on 7 Kamey. Twenty-five days later,
Alvarado and the army leave for Cuscatlan, defeating the people of
Atakat on 2 Kej along the way. Forty days later, on 10 Junajpu', Alvarado
returns to Iximche'. Tunatiw demands 1200 pesos' worth of gold within
five days. On 7 Ajmaq the Kaqchikel abandon Iximche'. Ten days later,
on 4 Kamey, they began their guerrilla war against the Spanish. Trenches
were dug, presumably to cut trails at strategic locations and thus impede
Spanish movement. Pitfalls lined with stakes are set as traps for Spanish
cavalry. On 4 Kamey, Alvarado has Iximche' burned. Later in the
account, on 6 Tz'i' the Kaqchikel begin to pay tribute.

This is a great deal of information to be conveyed in the spatially
constrained, minimalist format of the surviving pictographic annals
from central Mexico (such as the Codex Aubin, see Figure 6.1, p. 82)
and, as noted, the account's length and chronological detail contrast
dramatically with the other entries in the series. How could such detail

Figure 7.2   A simplified image based on the Tira de Tepechpan, illustrating the difficulty in attempting to portray wars and battles in an annals-history format.

have been recorded? An economical solution could have been a string of pictographs physically painted parallel to the main yearly account. However, such a string would have been awkwardly long and would need to have been lengthened further as developments occurred. The limitations of this option are suggested by entries in the Tira de Tepechpan (see Figure 7.2). Dotted lines were drawn from the relevant year dates to pictographic scenes of events in a given year. However, the quantity of detail is minimal and it would have been awkward indeed to convey a sense of a complex series of events occurring in a variety of places. A more likely possibility would have been a physically separate cartographic document appended to the annals account. The use of *Large subheadings with Wa'e* suggests the latter. Indeed, a cartographic account would have lent itself to easy updating as events unfolded during those chaotic times. New dates, characters, and place names could have been painted onto an existing map. This was exactly how the Xpantzay seem to have updated their cartographic history down through the 17th century (Maxwell and Hill 2006, 20–21).

Significantly, the Lienzo de Quauhquechollan depicts a parallel account from the point of view of Spanish indigenous allies from central Mexico who arrive in the Guatemala highlands in 1527. This massive cartographic history measures 3.25 by 2.45 meters, though it is estimated that as much as a third of the width was cut off at some point (Asselbergs 2004, 75; Universidad Francisco Marroquín 2007). As participants in the conquest campaigns, their account contains much more information concerning their movements and the numerous battles they fought along the way. Despite the lienzo's size it is ultimately a constrained format, given the amount of information it was intended to convey. Accordingly, the battle scenes themselves are very small, typically consisting of only two combatants. Even the largest battle scenes contain fewer than a dozen figures, all drawn at very small scale (see Figure 7.3). It would have been difficult at best for such scenes

Figure 7.3 A detail modified from the Lienzo de Quauhquechollan (Universidad Francisco Marroquín 2007), depicting series of battles in a longer campaign. Note the density of presentation that would have made it difficult to present the details of any one engagement.

Reproduced courtesy of the Universidad Francisco Marroquín and the Banco G&T Continental.

to convey more that the fact of a battle itself, its location and, through the addition of day signs (not present in the Quauhquechollan lienzo), the date on which it occurred. In any case, this lienzo demonstrates that important episodes spanning only a few years could be rendered in a cartographic account.

Excerpt from Maxwell and Hill (2006, 256–271).

Here, the Arrival of the Spanish People at Xe Tulul

¶ Suddenly this year, in truth, the Spanish people arrived.
　　In the twenty-ninth year arrived the Spanish people at Xe Pit, Xe Tulul.
　　On one Q'anel, the K'iche' Winäq died there because of the Spanish people.
　　Tunatiw Adelantado was the name of their lord who, in truth, defeated all the amaq's.
　　Their faces were not yet known.
　　Stelae were still greeted at this time.

¶ He arrived at Xelajub'
　　The K'iche' Winäq were dissolved unto death again there.

Then (,töq) were routed the K'iche' Winäq, all those who opposed the Spanish people.

Then (,öq) the K'iche' Winäq were destroyed before Xelajub'.

¶ Then (Töq) he arrived at the town of Q'umarkaa'j
　　Immediately, he was received by the lords.
　　Just then, suddenly, the lords were shackled by Tunatiw.

¶ On four K'at the lords Ajpop [and] Ajpop K'amajay were burned by Tunatiw.
　　Tunatiw's heart was no yet sated by war.

Soon came a messenger from Tunatiw to the lords, an order
      for warriors.
"Let the warriors of the Ajpo Sotz'il [and] Ajpo Xajil come here
      to kill the K'iche' Winäq!"Said Tunatiw's messenger to
      the lords.
Immediately, Tunatiw's orders were sent.

Then (‚öq), 400 warriors went to kill the K'iche' Winäq.
      Just those of the town went.
He did not require all the warriors of the lords.
Only [after] the warriors went for the third time [did] the
      K'iche' Winäq begin to pay tribute.

Then (‚öq) we went forth to bring Tunatiw here, you, my sons!

And Then, in Truth, He Arrived in Iximche' [presented] Here

On One Junajpu', the Spanish people arrived in the town
      of Iximche'.
Tunatiw was the name of their lord.
Immediately, Tunatiw was greeted by the lords B'eleje' K'at
      [and] Kaji' Imox.
Tunatiw's heart was good towards the lords when, in truth,
      he arrived in town.
There was no war.
Rather, Tunatiw was happy when, in truth, he arrived in
      Iximche'.
Thus it was when the Spanish people arrived long ago, you,
      my sons!
In truth, it was frightening when the arrived.
Their faces were not known.
The lords perceived them as divine beings.
We, your fathers, perceived them thus.
We who truly saw their arrival at Iximche'.

Tunatiw slepted in the Tzupam Jay.

The next day, the lord dreamt that a frightening number of
warriors came to him during his sleep.

He sent for the lords.

*"Why will you make war on me? Is there something I am doing
to you?"* said he.

*"It is not at all that way; it is just that many warriors have
died here.*

*It is they that you now see in the hole which is in the middle of
them,"* said the lords.

Thus, then he entered the house of lord Ch'ikb'al.

¶ Suddenly, Tunatiw asked the lords about enemies.

The lords said: *"I have two enemies; the Tz'utujil and those of
Atakat, you divine being,"* he was told by the lords.

Five days later, Tunatiw went out of the town to do it, when
the Tz'utujils died because of the Spanish people.

On seven Kamey, the Tz'utujils were killed by Tunatiw.

¶ Just twenty-five days later, he passed from the town to do it,
when Tunatiw went to Cuscatlan.

The [people of] Atakat died as he passed through.

On two Kej, the Atakat died because of the Spanish people.

All the warriors went with Tunatiw to kill the Yaki'.

On ten Junajpu', he came back, he returned from Cuscatlan.

Just forty days he was gone working over Cuscatlan when he
returned to town.

Then (,töq), Tunatiw asked for one of the daughters of the lords.

She was given to Tunatiw by the lords.

The Demand for Precious Metal [presented] Here

¶ Then (Töq) the lords' precious metal was demanded by Tunatiw.

100 PICTOGRAPH TO ALPHABET—AND BACK

Although he wanted to be given collected precious metal,
    truly, just gourds, just crowns, they brought nothing.
Tunatiw became angry with the lords.
He said: *"Why won't you give me precious metal?*
The precious metal of all the amaq's has not arrived here with
    you.
Do you want me to burn you, to hang you?" he said to the lords.

¶ Then (Töq) Tunatiw demanded 1,200 pesos in gold.
    The lords tried to have it reduced.
    The lords cried before him.
    But Tunatiw did not want it any other way.
    He just said:*" Hand over the precious metal!*
    You have five days to deliver it.
    If you do not deliver it then, you will know my heart!" the lords
        were told.
    Immediately, his wax seal was set down [on the order].

Then (,töq) the lords collected their precious metal
    And all the grandsons of the lords and the sons of the lords
        gave their precious metal.
    The people did what they could for the lords.

¶ In the middle of paying the precious metal to Tunatiw, a demon-
    man appeared.
    "I am thunder; I will kill the Spanish people!" he said to the
        lords.
    "They will be consumed in fire!
    Let me strike the town!
    Let the lords go across the river!
    Let it be on seven Ajmaq that I do this!" said the man, the
        demon, to the lords.
    In truth, the lords believed him.
    The man's words were obeyed by them.

In truth, the delivery of the precious metal was half completed when we dispersed.

In Truth, We Dispersed from the Town [presented] Here

¶ On seven Ajmaq the dispersal occurred
> Then the town of Iximche' was abandoned because of the demon-man
> Then the lords left.
> *"Now, in truth, will Tunatiw die!"* they said.
> There was no war in the heart of Tunatiw.
> He was happy because of the precious metal that he was being given.
> But, because of the man, the demon.

Then (,töq) the town was left abandoned on seven Ajmaq, you, my sons!

¶ The (öq) lords were missed, though, by Tunatiw
> Ten days after we dispersed from the town, the war began on account of the Spanish people.
> On four Kamey began our suffering, our dying on account of the Spanish people.
> Then started our suffering; we dispersed beneath the trees, under the vines, you, my sons!
> All [of us in] the amaq', we were in mortal combat with Tunatiw.
> At the height of it, the Spanish people departed.
> They left the town, they left it abandoned.

Then (,Töq) the Spanish people were opposed by the Kaqchikel Winäq.
> Trenches were dug.

Pitfalls for horses were made with stakes to kill them.

In truth, war was waged again by the people

Many Spanish people died.

So too did many of their horses in the pitfalls.

The K'iche' Winäq [and the] Tz'utujils were dissolved.

Thus, all the amaq's were dissolved because of the Kaqchikel Winäq.

And so, the Spanish people distinguished themselves.

Also, the amaq' distinguished itself.

8

Transition to Alphabetic Writing
in the Annals History

THE CARTOGRAPHIC MIGRATION history and res gestae portions of the Xajil Chronicle are complete historical accounts unto themselves. They need no additions or updating and could have been redacted through performance alone. On the other hand, the annals portion was an ongoing account carried through the Spanish conquest at least as far as the early 17th century. Although events of the preconquest years could have been rendered pictographically, postconquest events involving increasing numbers of Spaniards and Spanish vocabulary would have required a changeover to alphabetic writing. How and when did this process occur?

First of all, we should not expect that there was a sudden shift from pictographic writing in the annals or that such a shift was ever complete. As noted earlier, analogous documents from Mexico, such as the Codex Aubin (see Figure 6.1, p. 82), display a combination of both forms of writing, the relative importance of which changed over time. As Lockhart has noted in this regard:

> Thus in the Codex Aubin, as in preconquest practice, the pictorial component identifies the topic and gives some basic information; the alphabetic text, assuming the role of the preconquest oral component, repeats the information and expands upon it, giving many important details not portrayed pictographically . . . . As the years progress, the pictorials in the manuscript seem to bear ever less of the load of communication. They tend to become eye-catching topic indicators . . . while the alphabetic text becomes the primary medium. (Lockhart 1992, 351)

The Xajil Chronicle continues to include the anniversary dates of the Tuquche' revolt in the Maya calendar down through 1603. Other Maya day-dates occur sporadically as well and there are many examples of the same day rendered in both calendrical systems. The Maya dates could still have been rendered pictographically. However, from 1565 on the European calendar, months, weekdays, and feast-days had replaced the Maya system to organize the sequence of events within a given year, and presumably those words needed to be written alphabetically.

In terms of when the shift to alphabetic writing occurred, it is doubtful that any Kaqchikel would have been so instructed prior to the introduction of friar Francisco de la Parra's orthography in 1556. It is not a coincidence that the Chronicle entry for the following year, 1557, is the first in which the Spanish word "alcaldes" is used and the Spanish baptismal names of the Kaqchikel officeholders are entered. From this point on, the number of Spanish words in the text grows rapidly, denoting increasing alphabetization.

There is evidence to suggest that a literate scribe (probably Diego Hernández Xajil himself) returned to earlier annals entries to insert alphabetic information. For example, an entry for the year 1520 notes that the lord Jun Iq' died in an epidemic. The entry goes on to note that one of his sons, named "Francisco," survived, whereas one of the children of Jun Iq' by his first wife was the father of "Don Pedro Solís" (who became Ajpo Xajil in 1580) (Maxwell and Hill, 249–250). Diego Hernández Xajil's son "Diego" was born in 1527 (ibid, 276). Don Jorge and Don Juan Juárez are named in the 1532 entry (ibid, 281–282). Clearly, these are references to individuals who were born before or just after the conquest and who survived to receive baptism and Spanish names later, but before the appearance of the Parra orthography in 1556. Again, we have examples of later alphabetic notations to pictographic annals from Mexico. Spanish civil and ecclesiastical officials' names were also probably inserted later. For example, we see Archbishop Maldonado in the entry for 1535, friars Pedro Angulo and Juan de Torres in 1540, Juan Rogel in 1545, and President Cerrato in 1547.

Comparisons with Other 17th-Century Maya Manuscripts

The highly elaborate system of subheadings in the Xajil Chronicle is not found in any of the other 17th-century copies of 16th-century highland Maya alphabetic texts. We can detect only a few, modest parallels in these other texts and this makes determining their bases, oral and/or pictographic, highly problematic.

Popol Vuh

The text that has come down to us was written by Dominican friar Francisco Ximénez in the late 17th/early 18th centuries (Edmonson

1971, vii–ix). The elaborate use of serifs and töq/öq subheadings is lacking in the text, limiting us to speculation regarding its possible pictographic origins. One reason for the absence of the elaborate subheading structure may be attributable to the text's creation. The Dominicans preferred that friars residing in Maya communities compose their own summaries of mythological and historical accounts based on oral presentation by town elders. The resulting texts were to be used as aids for indoctrinating the Maya and to enhance subsequent friars' ability to detect any backsliding to preconquest practices (Remesal 1964, 419–420; Quiroa 2011). Their approach stands in stark contrast to the Franciscan practice (noted earlier) of encouraging the Maya to write the accounts themselves. Accordingly, Ximénez probably worked from documents written by friars who likely were not sensitive to the intricacies of Maya narration based on pictographic documents. This is reflected in the fact that punctuation occurs only sparsely and irregularly in Ximénez's text, making it difficult to detect possible subheading breaks within it. Ximénez's own parallel translation of the K'iche' to Spanish in columns on each page also must have affected his presentation of the text(s) to at least some degree. On the other hand, Ximénez did distinguish large divisions of the text, many of these beginning with "Wae.'" These divisions were reproduced in Munro Edmonson's translation with his insertion of Roman numerals (Edmonson 1971). However, this constitutes only one minor parallel with the Xajil Chronicle.

Título de Totonicapan

With the *Título de Totonicapan* we move from the careful handwriting of educated friars to that of Maya town scribes, about whose training we know almost nothing. We must suspect that town scribes, as public officials, had many other writing tasks to perform, so speed was an important consideration. Accordingly, their script is generally much less neat than Ximénez's and that of the Xajil Chronicle's copyist. Paper also was expensive, so scribes also had to contend with squeezing their texts into much smaller formats. Various kinds of errors also dot the

scribes' texts, suggesting limited training. Although the original alphabetic version of the *Título de Totonicapan* was composed in the mid-
16th century, Carmack and Mondlock estimate that the surviving document is a copy made between 1650 and 1725 and they recognize that
changes in the text must have occurred (Carmack and Mondloch 1983,
11). Indeed, the surviving copy may not even be the first one. A century
or more would have passed between the mid-16th and mid/late 17th
centuries so the possibility of an intermediate copy cannot be dismissed;
there is no way to estimate how much of an original textual presentation
might have been lost in a scribe's effort to copy it quickly. Punctuation
is limited to single or parallel double-dashes at the ends. Serifs predominate in subdividing the text and "Wae'" or "Are'" typically begin these
sections. The elaborate töq/öq subheadings of the Xajil Chronicle are
not paralleled in the K'iche' text. The equivalent K'iche' words "ta,"
"tak," or "take'" were employed only infrequently. Although the evidence is suggestive, again it is not possible to identify readily what
pictographic genre(s), if any, might have served as a basis of the alphabetic document.

Xpantzay Cartulary

The subheading structure of the Xajil Chronicle is not even found on
the other main 16th-century Kaqchikel texts contained in the Xpantzay
Cartulary. The six documents contained in the Cartulary were also
produced by indigenous scribes, and represent three different hands
(Maxwell and Hill 2006, 17–18). Of the corpus, only one appears
actually to have been written in the 16th century (specifically, 1581).
The others are all 17th-century copies of earlier documents. All but
one address topics that could easily have originally had pictographic
treatment. In terms of content, "The Origins and Lands of the Xpantzay"
is very much in the cartographic genre. The Töq/öq structure is not
present in the "Wars of the Sotz'il and Tuquche'," but also contains the
phrase "It is said," suggesting that this account is based on oral tradition
rather than a pictographic account.

9

Conclusions and Implications

To THE EXTENT THAT THE CASE has been made that we can indeed detect different types of pictographic documents in the Xajil Chronicle, the fundamental implication is that preconquest historians made use of a range of genres and formats, chosen according to the historical information and the desired level of detail in the accounts they prepared. Accordingly, we should expect that the leadership of a polity of any significance would have maintained essentially an "archive" in which these varied kinds of documents could have been kept, updated, referred to, and withdrawn for performance depending on the needs of a situation. The size and composition of such "archives" would naturally have varied according to the importance and age of the polity. In the case of the Xajil and Iximche', we have a family that extends back only a few generations before the timeless, "legendary" migrations of Q'aq'awitz and Saktekaw and a polity formed only a half-century before the Spanish arrival.

We might attempt to contrast the Iximche' case with the central Mexican polities, where greater time depth and/or political importance would have resulted in larger and probably more diverse "archival" collections. Some of their pictographic histories in postconquest, mixed-format pictographic documents extended back to the migration accounts situated in the late 12th century (for example, the Codex Mexicanus). With more time to cover and with a concern in tracing descent back to "Toltec" ancestors, we might expect multiple cartographic accounts of movements and events along the way, plus genealology, along with the careers of illustrious ancestors, all in absolute time. At the top of the size scale we have the huge archive of the regionally dominant Aztec polity at Tenochtitlan and the royal library of Texcoco referred to by later chroniclers. Even though Tenochtitlan achieved polity status toward the end of the latter part of preconquest times, it still did so a century and a half before Iximche'. The Aztecs' campaigns, battles, and other important events over this longer period would have been recorded in more detail through cartographic or other formats, as attested to by Díaz del Castillo (quoted previously, see pp. 87–88). We might also expect that as the Aztecs extended their hegemony they confiscated or copied the historical accounts of their subject polities as well.

Another implication is the possibility of gauging the extent of memorization required by indigenous historians to use or recount these documents. Although speech acts could be indicated pictographically through speech-scrolls emanating from figures' mouths, the content of an address or conversation could not. Hence, at a minimum, dialog would have required memorization. But speech is a relatively minor component of the Xajil Chronicle, so memorization was probably not particularly onerous, especially if we assume that no single individual had sole responsibility for all of the documents in the "archive." However, this is not to say that speech was inevitably a minor component in all pictographic histories. The events (including speech) that occurred at a specific locus on a large cartographic history would also have required memorization, because space constraints would have limited the information to only location and a few actors. Yet, as discussed earlier, indigenous historians seem to have had the flexibility to create additional cartographic documents (and presumably other formats as well) to record specific events in greater detail than a large-scale historical "outline" would permit.

Beyond these considerations, most other information in any historical format could have been conveyed readily through pictographs to an individual trained in their conventions and interpretation. Personal, group, and place names in surviving Mixtec and Nahua pictographic texts from central Mexico have long been readily decipherable by modern scholars. For cartographic histories, movement through space was recorded conventionally through passage from one named location to another and the names of leaders as representatives of entire peoples could easily be accommodated in the available space. With their focus on individuals, res gestae accounts and genealogies would also seem to have been largely decipherable for indigenous historians based on the pictographs alone, excepting the unkown variable of the importance of speech in the accounts. The time dimension in annals histories would have been straightforward, though space constraints would have resulted in rudimentary pictographic representation of the events to which they referred. Again, this limitation could have been mitigated when necessary by creating other documents in formats suited to record the event in more detail.

Works Cited

Asselbergs, Florine. 2004. *Conquered Conquistadors, The Lienzo de Quauhquechollan: A Nahua Vision of the Conquest of Guatemala.* Boulder: University of Colorado Press.

Boone, Elizabeth H. 1994. "Aztec Pictorial Histories: Records without Words." In *Writing without Words*, edited by Elizabeth Hill Boone and Walter D. Mignolo. Durham: Duke UniversityPress.

———. 1998. "Pictorial Documents and Visual Thinking in Postconquest Mexico." In *Native Traditions in the Postconquest World*, edited by Elizabeth Hill Boone and Tom Cummins. Washington, D.C.: Dumbarton Oaks.

———. 2000. *Stories in Red and Black*. Austin: University of Texas Press.

Boone, Elizabeth H., and Michael E. Smith. 2003. "Postclassic International Styles and Symbol Sets." In *The Postclassic Mesoamerican World*, edited by Michael E. Smith and Frances F. Berdan. Salt Lake City: Universityof Utah Press.

Brown, Cecil H. 1991. "Hieroglyphic Literacy in Ancient Mayaland: Inferences from Linguistic Data." *Current Anthropology* 32(4): 489–496.

Carmack, Robert. 1972. *Quichean Civilization*. Norman: University of Oklahoma Press.

———. 1979. "Arte Quicheano: Una Variante Mixteca-Puebla." *Historia Social de los Quiches*. Guatemala: Seminario de Integración Social.

———. 1981. *The Quiche Mayas of Utatlan*. Norman: University of Oklahoma Press.

Carmack, Robert, and James Mondloch. 1983. *El Título de Totonicapan.* Mexico, D.F.: Universidad Nacional Autónoma de Mexico.

Carrasco, Pedro. 1967. "El Señorío Tz'utujil de Atitlan en el siglo XVI." *Revista Mexicana de Estudios Antropológicos* 21: 317–333.

Castañeda de la Paz, María. 2006. *Pintura de la perigrinación de los culhuaque-mexitin (Mapa de Sigüenza)*. Zinacantepec, México: El Colegio Mexiquense.

Codex Aubin. 1893. *Histoire de la nacion mexicaine, depuis le départ d'Aztlan jusqu' a l'arrivée des conquérants Espagnols*. Paris: Ernest Leroux.

Coto, Thomás. 1983. In *Thesarus Verborum: Compendio de la lengua Cakchiquel u Guatemalteca*, edited by René Acuña. Mexico: Universidad Nacional Autónoma de México.

Díaz del Castillo, Bernal. 1956. *The Discovery and Conquest of Mexico*. New York: Farrar, Straus and Cudahy.

Edmonson, Munro S. 1971. *The Book of Counsel: The Popol Vuh of the Quiche Maya of Guatemala*. Middle American Research Institute Publication 35. New Orleans: Tulane University.

Fuentes y Guzmán, Francisco Antonio de. 1969–1972. In *Obras Históricas de don Francisco Antonio de Fuentes y Guzmán*. 3 tomos, edited by Carmelo Sáenz de Santa María. Biblioteca de Autores Expañoles. Madrid: Ediciones Atlas.

Guillemin, Georges, and Ferdinand Anders. 1965. "Ausgraben in Iximche': Ein Beitrag zur Kunst der Cakchiquel-Maya." *Wiener Völkerkundliche Mitteilungen* XII Jhg., N. N., Bd. VII: 73–83.

Hill, Robert M. II. 1996. "Eastern Chajomá (Cakchiquel) Political Geography." *Ancient Mesoamerica* 7: 63–87.

————. 2005. "Kaqchikel Chronicles as Redactions of Preconquest Pictorial Documents: A Review of the Evidence." Paper presented at the Annual Meeting of the American Society for Ethnohistory, Santa Fe, NM.

Keen, Benjamin. 1971. *Life and Labor in Ancient Mexico: The Brief and Summary Relation of the Lords of New Spain by Alonso de Zorita*. New Brunswick: Rutgers University Press.

Kirchhoff, Paul, Lina Odena Güemes, and Luís Reyes García. 1976. *Historia Tolteca-Chichimeca*. México, D.F.: CISINAH and INAH-SEP.

Leibsohn, Dana. 2009. *Script and Glyph: Pre-Hispanic History, Colonial Bookmaking, and the Historia Tolteca-Chichimeca*. Washington, D.C.: Dumbarton Oaks.

León-Portilla, Miguel. 1992. "Have We Really Translated the Mesoamerican 'Ancient World'?" In *On the Transformation of Native American Literatures*, edited by Brian Swann. Washington, D.C.: Smithsonian Institution.

Lockhart, James. 1992. *The Nahuas after the Conquest*. Stanford: Stanford University Press.

Maxwell, Judith M., and Robert M. Hill II. 2006. *Kaqchikel Chronicles.* Austin: University of Texas Press.

Monaghan, John. 1990. "Verbal Performance and the Mixtec Codices." *Ancient Mesoamerica* 1: 133–140.

———. 1994. "The Text in the Body, The Body in the Text: Embodied Sign in Mixtec Writing." In *Writing without Words*, edited by Elizabeth Hill Boone and Walter D. Mignolo. Durham: Duke University Press.

Nance, C. Roger, Stephen L. Whittington, and Barbara E. Borg. 2003. *Archaeology and Ethnohistory of Iximche'.* Gainesville: University Press of Florida.

Nuttall, Zelia. (1902) 1975. *The Codex Nuttall: A Picture Manuscript from Ancient Mexico.* New York: Dover Publications.

Quiroa, Néstor. 2011. "The Popol Vuh and the Dominican Religious Extirpation in Highland Guatemala." *The Americas* 74(4): 467–494.

Remesal, Fray Antonio de. 1964. *Historia General de las Indias Occidentales y particular de la Gobernación de Chiapa y Guatemala.* 2 vols. Madrid: Editorial Atlas.

Robertson, Donald. 1972. "The Pinturas (Maps) of the Relaciones Geográficas, With a Catalog." In *Handbook of Middle American Indians, Volume 12, Guide to Ethnohistorical Sources, Part One*, Howard F. Cline, volume editor. Austin: University of Texas Press.

Smith, Mary Elizabeth. 1973. *Picture Writing from Ancient Southern Mexico.* Norman: University of Oklahoma Press.

Troike, Nancy. 1982. "The Interpretation of Postures and Gestures in the Mixtec Codices." In *The Art and Iconography of Late Post-Classic Central Mexico,* edited by Elizabeth Hill Boone. Washington, D.C.: Dumbarton Oaks.

Universidad Francisco Marroquín. 2007. *Quauhquechollan, El lienzo de la conquista.* Guatemala: Universidad Francisco Marroquín.

Vázquez, Fr. Francisco. 1937–1944. *Crónica de la Provincia del Santísimo Nombre de Jesús de Guatemala* (4 vols.). Guatemala: Tipografía Nacional.

Wauchope, Robert. 1949. "Las Edades de Utatlan e Iximche." *Antropología e Historia de Guatemala* 1(1): 10–22.

Ximénez, Fray Francisco. 1973. *Popol Vuh* (edición facimilar). Guatemala: Editorial "José Pineda Ibarra."

Index